The Sky in My Hands

The Sky in My Hands

Accelerating Academic English through the Writing Process

Carol Irene Bearse

Language Learning Innovations, Inc.
Cambridge, Massachusetts

Published by:

Language Learning Innovations, Inc.
PO Box 380822
Cambridge, MA 02238
www.LLinnovations.com

Library of Congress Control Number 2005929527
Bearse, Carol I.

ISBN 0-9770825-0-4

Editor: Paula Leoni-Bacchus
Cover Design: Max Harless

Table of Contents

List of Figures

Acknowledgements

Every book is the result of years of inspiration and the practical wisdom of many colleagues. This one is no different. First, I wish to thank Paula Leoni-Bacchus of Language Learning Innovations for her belief in my work and her tireless efforts on my behalf. To Erich Schneiderman, thank you for your many hours of copy editing—you are amazing! To my colleagues at Lesley University who supported me throughout my dissertation process, which led ultimately to this book, thank you as well. Particular thanks to Dr. Solange Lira and Dr. Caroline Heller for their extraordinary work in helping me to shape my research into palatable form. Thank you, Caroline, for making qualitative research come alive for me.

Thanks also to Judith Steinbergh and Victor Cockburn of Troubadour for over twenty years of friendship through poetry and music. Our collaboration in creating The Student Writing Conference has been a source of constant joy and celebration for me and my students.

Last but not least, I wish to thank the countless teachers, students, and administrators I have worked with over the years. Thank you, Juan and Susan, for your creative leadership. To the teachers who have taken risks in their teaching, thank you for believing in the power and beauty of adolescent voices. To the urban, bilingual students who have inspired me, I cannot imagine my teaching life without you.

It takes a village and the love of a family to raise a child.

It takes another village to raise a writer and teacher.

Carol Irene Bearse
May, 2005

Editor's Preface

In the quietude, away from the noise and the shouting of the playground, away from the sirens and the tension of the city projects, these adolescents were reacquainting themselves with not only the beauty around them, but with the beauty within themselves. Just like Mary in the book *The Secret Garden,* who begged for a bit of earth, we all begged for a bit of sky that day on which to build our dreams. We all need the opportunity for tranquility where we can find the words to write our poems. Later, Alyssa wrote:

> *I have the sky in my hands but the twilight is just a simple purple flower….*
> *…and the sun is just a little buttercup.*
> *The clouds are just fluffy white flowers in my hand.*
> *That is the sky in my hands.*

This is what Carol Irene Bearse calls poetry of identity. It is also the starting point on a journey that connects her students' daily school experiences to their homes, their languages, their cultures, and their hearts. Carol's approach to teaching writing to multilingual students through poetry is thus grounded in the universal theme of finding oneself within the world, a world that often feels foreign and incomprehensible.

For adolescents, identity is a theme that occupies much of their thought. Young immigrants often experience radical transitions that can make this already-difficult stage of life seem overwhelming. This creates an even stronger need to explore identity and to talk about different worlds, home and language, losing and finding, and nostalgia and belonging.

Through case studies and a detailed account of her method and classroom experiences, Carol here shows how she creates a community of writers and readers in the classroom, how the students write their identities over weeks, months, and years, and how their development as successful writers of academic English is accelerated through poetry and through a variety of writing exercises. Ultimately, Carol's devotion to the adolescent multilingual writing experience develops into a collaborative model that involves co-teaching, demonstrating, modeling, and even a program for a School Writing Conference.

The Sky in My Hands takes us on a journey through two decades of Carol Irene Bearse's teaching and writing experiences. The result is a personal testimony and a guideline for writing teachers who want to make deeper connections and achieve more successful outcomes for English learners. Carol teaches students to build new futures by writing from their past experiences and their present memories. In the end, this leaves her students better prepared for the world of today.

Paula Leoni-Bacchus
Series Editor

CHAPTER 1

Introduction

The purpose of this chapter is to share with the reader the context of my growth as a teacher-researcher. This sociocultural context is important in understanding my philosophy of teaching second language learners—in particular my interest in the connections between adolescent writing and culture, language, and identity formation. On the whole, this book is a recounting of my three-year study in an inner city school in which 85% of the students were Latinos and second language learners of English. This study grounded all my further teaching experiences with second language learners in my present setting of a large suburban district with a very diverse population, with the largest population consisting of Latino/Brazilian students. I have used all the lessons discussed in this book in my teaching. I have been the Bilingual Curriculum Specialist for the Middle Schools in a system that has a strong Bilingual/Sheltered English/English as a Second Language (ESL) Program. I have grown in this position in our new context of high stakes testing, the No Child Left Behind (NCLB) Act, and new state English language proficiency exams. My research in writing through poetry about identity and cultural issues is still the basis for developing academic vocabulary for English language learners. In the program, the students move into personal and descriptive writing in the sixth grade. We have found that with this basis, students can move, with the help of a scaffolded, intense feedback approach, into the writing of a five paragraph essay that fulfills our state requirements in seventh grade. These requirements call for a composition based on a writing prompt that asks students for an informative narrative that is heavily descriptive. For the past two years, 92% of our English language learners have passed the state MCAS Language Arts exam.

This chapter begins with an account of my personal journey in literacy, followed by a rationale for the research, and then a discussion of the dialectic between theory and practice.

Personal Background

Literacy has always been important in my teaching. For ten years, I was a fourth and fifth grade classroom teacher. My elementary classrooms were infused with reading and writing, and my students engaged in literacy across all disciplines. As they researched and worked on projects together, these fourth and fifth graders actively constructed meaning from texts as they read. Concurrently, I found that their writing provided me with the best opportunity to see students' lives through their own eyes. Student's writing efforts also served as a springboard to encourage them to read and to explore authors' literary styles.

Because of the excitement generated around writing in my classrooms, and because I believe that teachers must become writers in order to teach writing, I decided to leave teaching at the elementary level for a few years to study writing in depth. I studied poetry writing through the Radcliffe Seminars and began my own consulting business as a Poet-in-the-Schools, in which role I taught all grades, K-12, for eight years. During this time infusing multicultural voices into diverse curricula became my passion. Some of the programs I developed included: "The Harlem Renaissance: Its Poets and Artists," "Chinese Poetry and Art," "The Poetry of the Netsilik Eskimo," "The Poetry and Music of Africa," "Poems in Two Voices in the Social Studies Curriculum," and "The Poetry and Art of Japan."

At the same time that I was a Poet-in-the-Schools, I worked as a language arts consultant for a public school in a suburb of Boston. In this capacity I worked with teachers to implement a whole-language reading program. By "whole language," I mean that the program taught literacy through authentic literacy events rather than isolated skills. I modeled lessons for teachers, held parent meetings, and worked with a committee to develop thematic units for the study of literature. I also led after school professional development workshops on topics related to children's literature and writing. As I worked with these students, parents, and teachers, I read widely in professional journals and began thinking about what new literacy questions were important for me. I wanted to find out more about the sorts of literacy that come out of children's experiences with the world around them. Another question that fascinated me was how students' reading of literature affects the writing of particular genres such as fairy tales or mystery stories.

Thus, in 1989 I began attending the Lesley College Summer Literacy Institutes and, concurrently, pursuing my certificate as a Consulting Teacher of Reading. Even though I loved literature and writing and considered myself a project-oriented teacher, I wondered how I could improve my teaching. How could I make literacy more student-centered? By this I meant, how could I implement constructivist learning in my classes? How could I reconcile theory with practice? These questions led me on a quest for books and articles by researchers who wrote about reading and writing workshops that centered on children's literature and on the choice of topics in both reading and writing. I began to be influenced by such authors as Nancie Atwell (1990), Lucy Calkins (1991, 1994), Donald Graves (l983), Jane Hansen (1987), and Donald Murray (1985, 1990). Louise Rosenblatt's (1978) theory of reading response and Lisa Delpit's (1991) research on the need for explicit instruction for minority students began, too, to guide my thinking. I began to think that the personal connection students made with texts could be optimally enlivened through their own meaning-making activities in reading and writing. Further, Delpit made me aware that minority students needed to be empowered with the "codes of power" that would propel their success in literacy through the uses of secondary discourses.

In the Lesley College program, I learned how to conduct reading research and found that I loved working in the library doing further reading to synthesize the many aspects of reading/writing studies that I'd already started to use in my practice. The questions that I wanted to continue to research concerned the relationship between reading and writing; in particular, I wanted to know more about how reading influences writing. My first published article for *The Reading Teacher* (Bearse, May, 1992) was a result of this initial research. This article described how third graders' readings of fairy tales affected their writing of fairy tales. This was my first attempt at synthesizing research, collecting data (in this case, samples of student writing), and drawing conclusions from the data. I didn't realize at the time that what I was doing was qualitative research and teacher-research. I called what I was doing "action research" because I found that by writing I was able to clarify my own thinking about teaching and apply these new ideas to my teaching practice.

Later, I became the Director/Teacher of an inner-city magnet school writing program (grades 3-8) in an urban school to the north of Boston where the student population was 85% Latino. Here, I had the unique opportunity to design a literacy curriculum for grades 3-8 based on identity, language, and culture. Because of federal funding, I also had the opportunity to order books and materials and develop a writing assessment program based on portfolio assessment that showed a student's growth over two three-year periods, grades 3-5 and 6-8. The portfolios were designed around collecting student writing that reflected specific genres in each grade, with benchmarks for success. In addition, the students at this school motivated me to learn Spanish in order to relate to their language and culture. Through this effort and my work with students, my thinking began to be dominated by the question of the connection between native language learning and the acquisition of a second language.

As we shared family stories, my students helped me to reclaim my own Greek urban roots. I shared with them my own writing about growing up with my *yaya*, my grandmother, and my mother, in a Greek tenement neighborhood and my pride in knowing two languages as a child. I became aware of the importance of language in the formation of identity, because I realized how growing up bilingual had become inextricably entwined with my identity.

I also remembercd growing up in Boston in the fifties. When I entered kindergarten, I was completely bilingual, but my teachers insisted that I only speak English. Although I felt that part of my identity was devalued, I wanted to become like the other monolingual children in my class. A part of me could always be hidden from the world because I had bright red hair and an English surname. However, I identified with my Greek roots because during my formative years from birth to three years old, I lived with my Greek grandparents and my mother while my English father was in the Navy. My "Greekness" was further embedded in me by being brought up in the Greek Orthodox Church, where I sang in the choir and studied and later taught in the Sunday school, thus maintaining my native language. Through understanding my adolescent English language learner students' identity formation as bilingual readers and writers, I have become more aware of who I am as a Greek American by remembering who I was as a bilingual child.

Through my experience in this urban school I learned that literacy has the capacity to empower inner-city students. By "empower" I mean to help students feel confident about the strength of their own voices to speak out and write about their own life experiences. They began to write about the inequities of racism that they faced every day. They became inspired by such diverse authors as Maya Angelou, Langston Hughes, Sandra Cisneros, Gary Soto, and Nikki Giovanni. These authors' lives and struggles reflected their own struggles as minorities in America.

My experience thus also re-awakened me to the inequities of class and culture. While at this school, I read and was influenced by Mike Rose's (1989) book *Lives on the Boundary*. Rose views teaching in terms of reaching across cultures and across class boundaries: "Culture and class erect boundaries that hinder our vision—blind us to the logic of error and the ever present stirring of language—and encourage the designation of otherness, difference, and deficiency" (p. 205). In order to understand literacy, I came to believe that we need to understand the sociocultural context in which we are teaching.

When the principal left the magnet school in 1994 to begin a new middle school in a diverse suburban community west of Boston, he invited me to be the Literacy Specialist in this school and to set up a new literacy program, and I accepted the position. At this writing, I am again working with a very diverse population, including Brazilian, Latino, Asian, African American, African, Indian, Pakistani, Chinese, Russian, Haitian, and Vietnamese students. From the beginning, I saw the need for an additional Advanced/Transitional ESL class (ESL V) within the Bilingual Department, which I created and taught. English language learners were struggling and failing to learn in the mainstream classes. These students needed, I believed, the additional support of an intensive English class while developing their writing skills in the mainstream content areas. They would take this course instead of an elective world language class. Within this context, I was able to observe closely the development of biliteracy and the difficulties these children experienced in learning academic English. I struggled daily with how best to improve my students' literacy skills and enhance their cultural identities. I also wanted to gain a deeper knowledge of Spanish so I could relive what it was to learn a second language—this time as an adult.

Thus, in the summer of 1995, I traveled to Costa Rica to study Spanish intensively and to live with a native family. I remember how tired I was by the end of the day, as I struggled to speak Spanish all day and to learn to conjugate verbs and acquire vocabulary by night. When I began to dream in Spanish and to write directly in Spanish, I knew that I had reached a breakthrough in my language development. Through my own struggles to learn, I also appreciated more fully how difficult school was for my students who were English language learners, and I was eager to bring this new knowledge and sensitivity into my classroom. In learning Spanish as an adult, I became acutely aware of many aspects of language acquisition that I had previously taken for granted. These insights helped me to understand the processing and developmental needs of my students.

As a recipient of a Fulbright Scholarship in the summer of 2000, I had the opportunity to live and work in Fortaleza, Brazil for six weeks. During this time I worked side by side with my exchange partner in a public secondary school where I was able to observe second language learners on a daily basis. In addition, I learned Portuguese, this time with my knowledge of Spanish as a resource. With the perspective of learning a second language from a comparative approach, I began to understand how the knowledge of the structure of one language can affect the process of learning the structure of another.

Armed with this new knowledge of language acquisition, I felt ready to incorporate more authentic literacy projects in my ESL V classroom. By "authentic," I mean research based experiences in which students explore questions of their own choosing in both literature and their own experiences in the community. I believed that these kinds of projects would accelerate the learning of academic English. My students were all mainstreamed except for this one language support class. They were also ninety percent Brazilian. Because of my experiences in Brazil, I knew that talk and cooperative learning were the most effective strategies to use with my students. In Brazil, I observed classrooms of as many as fifty-four adolescents in which friendships and a relaxed learning atmosphere were highly valued. Through these friendships and through talk, students worked together to accomplish a common task. With this class, then, I decided to incorporate more cooperative learning strategies and found that collaborative inquiry worked best with these students. Because of their need to talk and to cooperate in learning, they enjoyed working together and produced individual research projects with the help of their peers. Students, in Latino/Brazilian cultures are more successful in learning when their "interdependent self" is valued (Markus & Kitayama, 1991). I also found that developing structured writing frames and individual conferencing helped my students to succeed.

Because of this experience with my ESL V class, I wanted to examine more closely how English language learners acquire academic English through research and collaborative inquiry projects. I was also interested in the role of language and culture in the identity formation of these adolescents. In my role as the Bilingual Curriculum Specialist in our school, I am able to see students at different ESL levels who come from a majority Latino/Brazilian population. This opportunity has given me first hand experience observing students as they acquire a second language, in particular, students who have been partially mainstreamed. This interest led to my doctoral research, in which I studied English language learners researching topics of their own choosing over the course of one academic year (Bearse, 2003).

Definitions

Essential to understanding the framework of *The Sky in My Hands* are the definitions of key terms that have guided my thinking. I believe that the concepts denoted by the following terms are inextricably bound up with the processes of second language acquisition among adolescent English language learners.

Identity formation
In the context of this book identity formation is defined as

> ...a process of simultaneous reflection and observation, a process taking place on all levels of mental functioning, by which the individual judges himself in the light of what he perceives to be the way in which others judge him in comparison to themselves and to a typology significant to them. (Erickson, 1968, p. 22)

Zone of proximal development
Vygotsky defines the zone of proximal development as the distance between the actual developmental level as determined by independent problem solving and the level of potential development as determined through problem solving under adult guidance or in collaboration with more capable peers: "The actual developmental level characterizes mental development retrospectively, while the zone of proximal development characterizes mental development prospectively" (1978, p. 86).

Collaborative inquiry
In the context of this book, collaborative inquiry is the process by which students engage in learning through cooperation with their peers and their teacher within a community engaged in collaborative inquiry. Wells (2000) suggests that within the zone of proximal development all learning is in some way collaborative. Because the whole person is involved in joint activity, there is also an identity-forming effect to collaborative efforts.

Authentic literacy
Authentic literacy events are defined by Goodman and Goodman (1990) as events that have personal and significant meaning for the language user. Within these events, there are transactions between the reader and the text in which the reader is continuously solving new problems and building and extending psycholinguistic strategies.

Academic English
Within the context of this book following Gee (1989), academic English is defined as English that is part of a secondary discourse. Secondary discourses are those learned in such places as schools, work places, and government offices. These secondary discourses imply knowledge of the dominant culture. Literacy, in this view, is defined as a dominant literacy that is in control of a secondary use of language.

Rationale for Research

The issues that affect bilingual and English language learners at the secondary level are among the least examined aspects of education in the United States (Faltis, 1999). This is particularly significant because, despite this gap, English language learner secondary school students are rapidly increasing in numbers. According to the U.S. Bureau of the Census (1990), one in every six middle and high school students spoke a language other than English at home, was a newcomer to this country, or both. Data also suggest that foreign-born children are concentrated in the upper age groups. According to the U.S. Bureau of the Census (1993), of children aged five to eighteen years old, only thirty-three percent of the foreign-born were five to ten years old, as compared to forty-five percent of native-born children who fell into that age range. The same data also indicated that more foreign-born than native-born youth fell into the age group between fourteen to nineteen years of age (see Rong & Preissle, 1997).

There is little debate about the need to improve the literacy skills of linguistically and culturally diverse student populations. According to the National Assessment of Educational Progress (NAEP), writing assessment data continue to reveal the poor writing achievement of this segment of the population, particularly among Latino students. For example, in grades eight and twelve, according to the NAEP, slightly less than fifty percent of the Latino students demonstrated minimal competence, whereas seventy-five percent of White students wrote minimally competent adequate responses (Gutierrez, 1992). Other studies have cited Latinos as constituting seventy percent of the LEP population in the United States (deFelix, Waxman, & Page, 1993). Scholars have recently reanalyzed Census Bureau figures and have determined that Latinos will account for most of the overall population growth between 1982 and 2020. In fact, it was estimated that in 1982 one in ten children was Latino, while one in four will be Latino in 2020 (deFelix, Waxman, & Paige, 1993). From these statistics, one can see the crucial importance of understanding what I call the "literacy learning lives" and, through this, the literacy needs of these students.

Furthermore, while there are countless studies of the writing process of monolingual students of all ages (Graves, 1983; Dyson, 1989; Emig, 1971, etc.) and a growing number of studies of learning to write in a second language (Valdés, 2001; Reyes, 1991), most studies of secondary school writing focus on measuring the development of writing through the use of dialogue journals (Peyton, 1990; Reyes, 1992; Hudelson, 1988; McLaine, 1986). These researchers have taken a micro-look at the products of writing, not the process of writing itself. Furthermore, Reyes (1991, 1992) found, based on her study of the writing process, that a more direct approach that includes explicit instruction and scaffolding can help English language learners move forward in their writing of English.

Because culture plays a key role in identity formation for bilingual adolescents, it may also play a pivotal role in the development of adolescent writing. This is often evident in bilingual adolescents' participation in multiple discourses. In this regard, Valdés (1999) refers to the need to pay attention to what students bring with them into the classroom, particularly in terms of their home cultures and the understandings they have developed about written language.

There is a need, then, to look at adolescent second language writing through the lens of a multiplicity of discourses. If writing development can be deduced to be a process of growth in social context, then the cultural, contextual, and individual differences of English language learners need to be better understood if educational theories and practices are to be relevant to helping second language students become more competent writers (see Cumming, 1998).

Building upon my doctoral research, this book extends the work of Mercado (1993) and Mercado and Moll (2000) by looking at the writing process from a Vygotskian perspective while examining the impact of culture and identity on this process. According to Nevarez-LaTorre (1999), given the changing population trends in urban settings, there is a growing need for teacher-research in classrooms where English language learners are taught, and for teacher-research in linguistically diverse settings:

> These trends demand comprehensive and innovative educational approaches that will promote knowledge produced by teachers to facilitate academic success for all students and build the understanding about effective practice in bilingual education settings. The involvement in teacher-research by practitioners who work with linguistically diverse students is one way to respond to the demands brought forth by such changing demands (p. 456).

Researcher Jim Cummins (1996) interprets Vygotsky's zone of proximal development to be the interpersonal space in which minds meet and new understandings can arise through collaborative interaction and inquiry. This definition points clearly to the affective side of language acquisition and the importance of choice and motivation in developing literacy in a second language. Cummins points out that Newman, Griffin, and Cole (1989) label this interpersonal space as a "construction zone." Cummins elaborates this by saying, "Teacher-student collaboration in the construction of knowledge will operate effectively only in contexts where student identities are being affirmed" (1996, p. 26).

Listening to student voices
According to Nieto (1994), few studies have addressed the perceptions of Latino youth as they pertain to their American schooling experience, or their thinking, attitudes, and beliefs about school. Throughout *The Sky in My Hands*, you will hear students talk about the importance of writing in their lives and about the reasons behind their choice of writing topics. Torres-Guzmán and Thorne (2000) believe that studies investigating the voices of Latino students are critical to educational reform and school restructuring and may provide insight into the structures that perpetuate the underachievement and school failure found in Latino communities. This belief led to their study of an alternative bilingual/bicultural high school in a poor urban neighborhood where the dropout rate was 60-65%. They interviewed fifteen students over the period of one year about their perceptions of the schooling experiences. The following major issues emerged from these interviews:

- Teacher caring was associated with students' willingness to learn and put more effort into their work.

- Caring was a central value expressed by all students. Good teachers were caring, showed respect, and were supportive of students.

- Teacher caring was also shown by valuing the students' languages and cultures. The students wanted more inclusion of their cultures and languages in the curriculum and wanted teachers to learn about their cultures.

- A sense of humor and openness is important to a relaxed, familial atmosphere in the classroom.

- Student-teacher relationship and open communication are vitally important.

The role of teachers

As discussed above, the role of teachers is critical to the school success of Latino students. Hidalgo (1992) asserts that because of the value placed on interpersonal relationships in Latino culture, the relationship between the teacher and Puerto Rican student is vital to the educational achievement of the student. Nieto (1999) agrees: "Latino youngsters explicitly mention 'love' as the factor that can make or break their experiences in school" (p. 68).

Chavez (1997), writing about achieving equity for Latino students, declared that teachers must play a central role in developing relationships with their students that are rooted in respect, dignity, and high expectations. He states, "In essence, the Latino learner should be at the center of learning through a responsive pedagogy that promotes academic learning, social responsibility, and a proactive engagement by the politics of identity" (p. 9).

Similarly, Romo and Falbo (1996) conducted a three-year study of students of Mexican origin who were labeled "at risk" of dropping out by a school district. The data from this study reiterated the central importance of the teacher-student relationship. Likewise, Lucas (1993) stated that successful teachers of Latino students are those who are willing to try innovative practices and make their teaching culturally relevant. These teachers also encourage students to use their native language as needed for communication and interaction about course content, both among themselves and between students and teachers. Finally, and most importantly, they recognize student success overtly and frequently.

Salient curriculum features

Other researchers have examined curriculum designs that support the academic achievement of Latino students (Huerta-Macias, 1998; Mercado, 1993; Garcia, 1993; Lockwood & Secada, 2000). The common features of these curriculum designs are that they are student-centered, involve student choice, are project-centered, and include collaborative learning approaches.

For example, Mercado and Moll (2000) engaged a sixth grade bilingual class in an ethnographic research project in order to evaluate the students' reading achievement. The authors' approach was to enlist students as collaborators in the construction of the curriculum and to include students' home communities in their ethnographic research. Among the findings of this study was that students made significant gains on standardized reading tests within a seven-month period. As students used literacy for real purposes, they were able to engage in multiple discourses, including the discourse of researchers. They also learned to recognize and value knowledge discovered in their own homes as they collaborated with their parents on their research.

One case study was especially striking. In answer to the question, "How has research helped you to be a better learner?" Indio (the student) replied, "Research has helped me find my true inside...the one that cares" (p.126). Thus, students such as Indio created new identities as learners primarily though varied uses of writing, which included field notes, reflections, letters, reports, and presentations. As Van Manen (1990) explains: "Research is the work of writing, but in writing, the writer...produces more than text. The writer produces himself or herself.... Writing is a kind of self-making or forming" (p. 126).

Mercado (1993) examined how participation in an activity-based program influenced writing among young adolescent students who were predominately bilingual Latinos. Students in this project used the literacy practices of ethnographic researchers to learn about topics of personal interest. Sixth graders from one teacher's class were chosen for this study, which spanned a period of three years. Based on her in-depth analysis of five case studies, Mercado found literacy to be "an important means of coming to understand while at the same time affirming and transforming personal, ethnic, and linguistic identities" (p. 1).

Several major themes emerged from this project: 1) the uses of power literacies in inner city schools; 2) the use of literacy in the community; 3) having something to say and wanting to write; 4) changes in writing; and 5) what writing reveals about biliterate students. Because of the nature of research-related practices, these kinds of literary discourses have a powerful potential to help students become better learners. Mercado states: "Not only do students gain a new perspective on the importance and utility of writing, but they also begin to see themselves as writers and to understand that writing is a social responsibility for individuals who come from marginalized communities" (1993, p. 26).

Gersten and Jiménez (1999) reviewed research in the fields of cognitive strategies, approaches to teaching literature, and programs in bilingual education and second-language acquisition to develop specific suggestions for English learners. They identified eight constructs of effective instruction: challenge, involvement, success, scaffolding, mediation or feedback, collaborative/cooperative learning, techniques for sheltered English instruction, and respect for cultural diversity. Freeman and Freeman (2002) saw these constructs as interacting and overlapping with each other to provide successful experiences for Latino students.

Similarly, Saunders, O'Brien, Lennon, and McLean (1999) identified four theoretical premises to promote first- and second-language acquisition and academic achievement. These premises are as follows:

- Challenge: Consistently challenge students academically.

- Comprehensiveness: Address both meaning and skills, promote both higher level thinking skills and practice, and provide complimentary elements of student and teacher centeredness.

- Continuity: Achieve continuity in curriculum as students move from Spanish to English language arts.

- Connections: Build upon and make explicit the connections between students' existing knowledge and experiences and the academic content.

Finally, the fact that some students are limited in their English proficiency does not mean that they are limited in their thinking ability. These students must be pushed to engage with challenging ideas. Valdés (2001) found that the curriculum given to the English learners she studied was neither challenging nor comprehensive, and that as a result students were not prepared to enter mainstream classes. Valdés stressed the importance of giving students access to the curriculum while they are learning English.

A Framework

The above research lays the foundation for the chapters that follow, which describe how writing transformed the lives of certain inner city middle school students over a period of three years. Chapter Two describes an experience in which students speak informally about their growth in writing. Chapter Three provides further insight into student voices through three longitudinal studies of students discussing their writing growth. Chapter Four describes the poetry of identity technique, which builds the foundation of prose writing. Chapter Five moves on to the development of prose writing through personal narrative in grade six. Chapter Six presents the methods of oral history and writing for justice in grade seven. Chapter Seven extends these techniques to a further exploration of students' identities through memoir writing in grade eight. Chapter Eight describes the development of poetry writing in Spanish in the bilingual classes that I visited. Chapter Nine takes the reader to a Writing Conference that celebrates students' yearlong poetry writing in a unique conference format. Finally, Chapter Ten concludes by examining how poetry can enhance students' connections to the content areas.

CHAPTER 2

The Sky in My Hands

On a glorious spring day, Alyssa and I were walking in the woods as part of a sixth grade field trip. She noticed a blue aster, which she picked and cradled in her hands.

"Mrs. Bearse, look, I'm holding the sky in my hands!"

"Yes, you are, Alyssa. Not only are you holding the sky in your hands. Today I know that you have become a poet!"

Alyssa, a quiet, introspective student, was thrilled. Her face beamed. She answered, "You know, writing poems was hard for me at first. I didn't think I could do it; I just couldn't get the words right. I think I'm finally getting better at it."

Our conversation was interrupted by the excited calls of the rest of the group in front of us. We rushed forward to see what they had found.

"Look at this yellow flower. What's it called? It's so delicate," exclaimed Jessica.

"It's a buttercup. At least, that's what my grandmother called them."

"Look at this rock," José declared. "It's filled with dots!"

As we walked along the trail, other students called to each other about finding buttercups and odd shaped leaves. In contrast to the loud voices they used in school, here they whispered almost reverently to each other. They pointed out birch, maple, and oak trees; they noticed moss and stones underfoot. We held onto our treasures as we learned to discover the woods like poets: as keen observers, we were collecting all these sensations for our writing class. My students were helping me to rediscover the woods through their eyes; I was touched by their innocence and their captivation with the woods. In the quietude, away from the noise and the shouting of the playground, away from the sirens and the tension of the city projects, these adolescents were reacquainting themselves not only with the beauty around them, but with the beauty within themselves. Just like Mary in the book *The Secret Garden* (Burnett, 1998), who begged for a bit of earth, we all begged for a bit of sky that day on which to build our dreams.

We all need the opportunity for tranquility so we can find the words to write our poems. Later, Alyssa wrote:

> *I have the sky in my hands but the twilight is just a simple purple flower….*
> *…and the sun is just a little buttercup.*
> *The clouds are just fluffy white flowers in my hand.*
> *That is the sky in my hands.*

Renewal and Awakening

That spring was not only glorious for its beauty, with its yearly rebirth of color and warmth; it was glorious because it symbolized for me the renewal of my innermost beliefs about teaching and about the power of words to transform students' lives. During my twenty-five years as a classroom teacher, a Poet-in-the-Schools, a consultant teacher of reading and a bilingual curriculum specialist, I have come to believe that love and a passion for literature and writing can be powerful agents for transforming students into eager learners and motivated writers. A genuine love and respect shown to students by their teacher can transform apathetic adolescents into students who believe in their inner voices and their capacity for greatness. Over the years, these beliefs have been at the core of my philosophy of teaching. My urban students reaffirmed these ideas.

Later that spring, at the end of sixth grade, the inclusion class teachers asked their students to write notes or poems about what they had learned in writing class that year. Tough, street-wise Alex wrote: "She believes in us so she is a very important person to us. I enjoy her company even though we have her for forty-five minutes. Those forty-five minutes are fun, working and learning, but fun." Charles, an African American student whose general frustration frequently landed him in fights, echoed Alex's words: "I have learned a lot of things. I mainly thank you for being here and caring. You believe in all your kids that you have helped throughout the year. You also cheer kids on. Take Gilberto, for instance. He says he can't do it, he doesn't know how. Mrs. Bearse, you have helped Gilberto."

Alex and Charles were not unlike many of the students in my classes. They struggled to find the words and sentences to express themselves. Dana barely wrote the first six months of class; sometimes I would take dictation from her, because the physical act of writing was difficult for her. Sometimes I would let her draw first until she felt comfortable enough to write something in her journal. Back and forth between students, cheering them on, urging them to find the words. Julio, who loved to slick his hair back, dared me every day to get him to write. More often than not, he disrupted classes and his inclusion teacher would either sit by him or take him into the hall to write. He swore up and down that he had nothing to write about, but, little by little, he would write a few sentences; he might try a simple five sense poem describing the classroom or himself. Five lines were about all he could manage but we cheered his every step. Though struggling with obstacles and his own resistance, Julio was very perceptive. He never missed a trick; he absorbed everything that was going on around him and compensated for his difficulty with reading by observing and listening to stories and poems read aloud. When I asked his class in June to write about how they write their poems, he startled us all with the following:

How I Write My Poems

A poem is like a bird.
When a bird makes a nest, it is hard.
When a man writes a poem, it is hard.
A man can't make a nest.
A bird can't write a poem.

For Julio, writing was hard; he, like many other special needs students who have been in my classes, surprised us with the connections that he made. "Special needs," to me, has always meant that these students see the world in unusual ways and that as teachers we need to find alternative and multi-sensory approaches to help them learn. By its very nature, poetry is an alternative way of looking at the world. Because of Julio, I will never look at a bird or a birds' nest in the same way.

Insights and written evaluations by students like the above help inform my teaching and convince me that, for adolescents, *what* we teach is not as crucial as *how* we teach. For teachers of writing, all the magic we need can be found in books and in the passion in our voices. This is what our students remember. All too often, however, we get so bogged down by curriculum and paperwork that we forget why we became teachers in the first place. Students like Charles, Alyssa, and Julio help to remind me. With their help, we need to remind administrators, school committee members, and parents that literacy is about creating hopes and dreams. With words we can make learning happen for our students and give them something to look forward to.

Challenging the Statistics

Becoming poets is something I believe can free young adolescents like Alyssa and my other inner city students to become engaged in literacy and writing. Luckily, our principal at the time, a dynamic Hispanic leader, also believed in the capacity of writing to empower students' lives. He wanted to turn around the previous years' statistics: students had scored three years below grade level on state testing and substantially below that on nationally normed tests. He knew that if we could have the school designated a magnet school we could use the much needed funds to provide resources, books, and training for staff and students, the majority of whom spoke English as their second language. He also wanted to establish a Writing/Publishing Center as the core of the school, where teachers could find resources and students could publish their writing on computers.

The particular urban setting was an old mill city in northeastern Massachusetts that had seen its mills close and its jobs disappear. It had also seen a new wave of immigrants from Puerto Rico, the Dominican Republic, Vietnam, and Cambodia flood its schools. The school district was struggling to come up with the financial resources needed to repair dilapidated buildings and provide resources for its overcrowded classrooms. A forty-five percent high school drop-out rate, drug and gang violence, and disrupted families living at the poverty level were some of the social issues that the administration presented to me. The challenge was clear. Could we make learning meaningful under these conditions? Robert Frost said that a poem is a momentary stay against the confusion of the world. With poetry on our side, I believed that amazing things could happen. With poetry on our side, we could begin to take the risk of rediscovering ourselves.

Poetry: Crawling Inside Our Lives

To crawl inside our lives is often painful, but I knew that my students had many poems and stories buried within them. In their short lives, they had experienced more about the essence of living than I would ever experience. More often than not they had to be nudged to believe that they had stories worth telling: "You have stories and poems inside you. Your lives are filled with the sensory details of living. Write about what you know; write about what you care about. Get inside yourself. Speak out about what's on your mind."

Patrice, a seventh grade Haitian student, was often in trouble with her classroom teacher. She spoke out in class, she was late finishing assignments, she loved to goof around, and she had a sharp tongue that could wither the best of us. But Patrice loved writing poems about issues; she also told me that she loved writing songs and kept a journal at home. Her best poems were those that came from her thoughts about what was going on around her:

The ground is cracked from the tears through the night.
Sounds like the raindrops, pitty-patting along the roadside.
The silent prayers of children hungry and cold.
People wishing to be out of prison, to be set free, and not to be sold.
Women getting raped and see what kind of baby,
One that had no daddy and hides her tears.
But you see it isn't working.
They say it's better living here, but
for them they feel like croaking.
Trying to run away from their problems is what they try to seek.
And in the end, you realize you were blind and couldn't see.

For Patrice, this was the kind of writing she had to do. It was hard for me to imagine that a thirteen year old could have so much insight inside her. She taught me that time in writing class had to be reserved so that she could write these sorts of poems. Even though her teacher often argued with me that poetry wasn't going to help his students write "essays," I knew in my heart that I had to win the trust of my students before they could write more structured pieces. They had to have an opportunity to write about the issues that were bothering them. If I could "hook" them early with poetry, I knew that persuasive, descriptive and narrative writing would soon follow.

My vision, then, was to establish poetry as the link to other forms. Poetry could become the route to story for my students; once they felt successful in writing clear, concise poetry, they would risk writing longer pieces of prose. Poetry would enable adolescents to crawl inside themselves, and find the core of stories that were yet to be born. Learning that their experiences, their lives were important, they could share their common humanity with each other. They discovered, too, that all families had their share of problems and celebrations. As Lisa said, after writing her oral history, "I got to learn a lot about my mother.... We had a good conversation about our country and our family. This story brought a lot of memories from when I was young. I love this story because it comes from the heart."

Even in just one year, my students developed from hesitant writers to enthusiastic authors; they developed a love for poetry and books. When the students responded to a survey in June about their favorite kinds of writing, a typical response was: "Poetry, because it comes from the heart." My students confirmed what I had always believed: that children have a special relationship to language and to poetic thought; they respond to poetic insight as a way of sorting out and explaining their relationship to human experiences (Lewis, 1966). Through poetry, kids can give voices to those whose voices usually don't find their way into classrooms, including themselves (Christensen, 1991). In particular, I believe that urban adolescents speak with brutal honesty about the social issues that surround their lives; poetry is a means of empowering their voices to speak out with clarity and sensitivity on these and other topics.

Through writing, my students could also take control of the chaos around them by speaking out against the racism and violence they experienced. Most importantly, these adolescents learned that they could be masters of their own decisions. Andre put it best:

> *As I emerged into a teenager, everything changed. I faced a lot of problems with my family that year. My grandfather died and my grandmother moved away. Everything, all those feelings and the anger I felt were all trapped inside of me. I decided to give writing a chance. It was one of the best decisions I ever made. Even I was surprised to see what I can do as a writer. Writing took away all the anger, without me being violent, and it helped keep my secrets safe. Now I write all the time, for fun and when I'm feeling down. I now feel writing is a part of me.*

Andre wrote this at the end of eighth grade. I felt privileged that I was able to watch Andre grow from a hesitant sixth grader into an eloquent young man who went on to win a scholarship to a private prep school.

Andre's words haunted me. How could I explain to others the importance of writing in keeping adolescents "secrets safe?" How could I explain the liberation that students feel when they know that they can express their innermost feelings through writing? This book is the result of my search for answers to these questions; it is an attempt to recall my students' voices. I will never forget the beauty and intensity of these students' poetry in contrast to the grim realities that surrounded many of their lives growing up in the city. I will never forget the musicality of the Spanish language, which they helped to teach me. These gifts are immeasurable.

Program Design

As a mentor teacher visiting classrooms with over thirty students, many of whom had very special emotional and educational needs, it was imperative that I gain the trust of classroom teachers if I expected them to be willing to risk change. Beginning with small writing projects, including poetry, we demonstrated that students could be successful in these endeavors and were capable of learning. Designing my lessons to be teacher-directed and based on a flexible structure that could be replicated gave teachers a way to begin to use writing in their classrooms. The classes also revolved around the celebration of children's lives, so students could choose their writing topics within a broad theme or genre. I hoped that, little by little, classes would become more child-centered as both teachers and students became empowered to make more meaningful use of language and books. My design, then, was based on a conscious decision to balance choice and direct instruction to fit the context of my situation.

Teachers soon began calling me the "bag lady," as I entered classrooms with African straw bags filled with books, construction paper, and loads of markers. Entering classrooms became an event in itself, because of the physical layout of the building. The school was a series of separate blue buildings with high windows and flat-topped roofs, in the style of many buildings built in the 1950's. Each room had connecting doors to the next room and two to the outside; the inner courtyard was an overgrown sunken area that filled with water after heavy rains. On warm autumn and spring days, this kind of arrangement could be quite wonderful, but on rainy, snowy, winter days, I did a lot of traveling with my coat and umbrella along with my bags of books and materials. There were always eager kids to help me, though. They enjoyed being part of the procession of materials that entered the classroom! Classroom entrances became a ritual that grew out of necessity, but I noticed that these flurries of activity helped to generate the excitement that should come with writing.

Every writing lesson began with my reading of several picture books and the sharing of poems; students, even the most reticent, sat attentively through the reading of stories—in fact, they fairly gobbled the words up. For those who were second language learners, this language rich environment was vital to their growth as writers; they needed time and discussion to build the verbal background out of which to express themselves. And there was always art to induce the most reluctant to complete a final draft that could be illustrated and glorified with color. While on lunch or playground duty, students often stopped me, pleading, "Are you coming to our classroom today, please, missey?" Teachers, too, appreciated the infusion of materials that appeared with each writing lesson. Markers, watercolors, and scissors were a cause for celebration.

As the enthusiasm spread, more teachers began asking for writing lessons. Another magnet teacher was hired to work with the third through fifth grades, while I continued to focus on the mainstream and inclusion sixth, seventh, and eighth grade classes. Slowly, I began to work with the bilingual classes on a weekly basis to share my love of García Lorca and Spanish poetry. I remember commenting to the principal how tired my brain was after those classes, as I struggled to translate from English to Spanish, frantically looking up words in my dictionary. He laughed knowingly, "Now you know how hard it is for your students!" This comment has always stayed with me to inform my teaching of bilingual students. I can readily empathize with how tired their brains must be as they struggle to find the words in English.

It's the words that sing, they soar and descend.

Like the Chilean poet, Pablo Neruda, my students taught me that words sing. Words can help us soar like eagles when we're happy, and they can soothe us when we're afraid and confused. I depend on my students for insights that help me teach; their voices inform my teaching and brighten the world in which we live:

My Voice
My voice is a light to the world.
Cutting like a knife through the dark of the world.
My voice is an alarm clock of the world.
Waking people up to the problems that must be solved.
My voice is a rainbow of colors over the world.
Showing there is more than one color.
My voice is a ray of sun shining on the world.
Warming the world with the warmth of love.
My voice sounds loud, and it will be felt.

   Angela

Angela's poem is a wonderful transition to the next chapter, which presents a case study of three students describing their writing growth and showing that they, indeed, have voices that light up the world.

CHAPTER 3

WHO AM I? Three Longitudinal Studies

Who am I?
I'll tell you who I am.
I'm a thickheaded person, you know
some things don't go into my head right.
The fuzziness messes up my eyesight.
I'm fun to be with, I'll make you laugh and shout,
I'll show you what fun is all about.
I'm so sensitive, I'm always hurt deep in my heart,
I'll cry and cry until my heart falls apart.
I'm understanding because, my honey, I've been around.
I'll take care of any deepened frown.
I'm a good writer, I'll show you the world through my eyes.
I'll capture the moment and show you the biggest surprise.
I'm patient, as you can see,
I'm trying to tell you all about me.
I'm a dancer with toes so light and pretty,
With painted faces to show you my witty.
I'm a confident person so I do as I please,
I'm my own person, so strong you'll fall to your knees.
I'm trustworthy, no I won't let you down.
I'll carry all your secrets with me all around.
I'm honest I swear, I cannot tell a lie,
But this poem must come to an end and
I'll say it again, 'Exactly Who Am I?'

Elana asks in this poem the question that all adolescents ask themselves, "Exactly Who Am I?" Through their writing, adolescents have helped me to understand them a little better. I've learned about their ups and downs and their worries and fears.

In the three years that I worked with Elana, I observed her growth in writing as well as her increased ability to articulate her passion for writing. Through her portfolios, surveys, and informal interviews, she shared invaluable insights about the meaning of writing in her life. Elana stands out as a student who found her voice over time; in eighth grade, she became a leader in her classroom by inspiring other students to emulate her. She was also a member of my after school writing group for two years; this small group met once a week to share their projects or to continue the writing we had done in class. Most importantly, as Alyssa, another group member, once wrote, it was "a quiet place where [students could] write, away from the noise at home." Like Angela, Charles, and Julio, Elana renewed my belief that writing can become a central force in adolescents' lives.

ELANA: "Writing helps me express my feelings and get through another day."

When I met Elana in sixth grade I never would have guessed how important writing was to become in her life. I also would never have imagined that Elana would become one of the most prolific writers in our school. When I asked Elana to gather together all her writing from grades 6-8, she presented me with her journals, writing folders, published books, typed poems and stories. She had attached to many of these sticky notes indicating grade level and favorite pieces of writing. Beyond the school portfolios, she had compiled many of her own journals and collections. She showed me

Telling

The storm was frightning.

Showing by the 5 senses

I saw lighting reaching the tops of houses. The storm was so horrible houses beganlosing electricity one by one down the street. Heavy winds started collapsing the trees down to the hard ground. I heard the thunder that gave me quivveis up + down my spine. The noises of the raindropps bomming on the windowsill frighnened me. The smell of burnt up wires filled my bedroom I suddenly massaged away the fog on the window. I could almost taste my fear of the storm.

Figure 1: Elana's Paragraph about Lightning

her latest endeavors, which included poems based on interviews with her friends, stories and poems about abortion, having babies, abuse, boyfriends, and life in the city. She was also working on a longer autobiographical account containing poems and memoirs. Elana is a committed writer, one who writes every day in school and out of school. Writing has become a way of life for her.

At the end of their eighth grade year, I asked all my students how they had grown in writing from sixth to eighth grade. Here are some excerpts from what Elana wrote:

> *Well, I've always written long pieces of writing. But as I look into my folders I see a great change in the way I write.*
>
> *My lead sentences have grown greatly. They're no longer how a story starts, but the actual way it started in my mind.*
>
> *My details are more captivating. My vocabulary has increased greatly. People lock onto my poems with more interest and wonder because now I don't lead them into a place where stories or thoughts occur, but now I bring them into a world that's more involved. A wondrous world of pain, love, hate, and happiness.*
>
> *That's another thing I've grown in. Poets don't look at the world as "a world" but an imaginable place where the stars sing, and our mother is our earth, our trees our suppliers. A poet can talk to dirt, rocks, and the ocean....*
>
> *My sweetness is writing poems, but I've learned to open my heart even wider and share with the world. Now I also write short stories on how I feel. I've just completed a memoir also which improved my skills very much.*

I am impressed with Elana's perception of her growth as a writer. She acknowledges the need to have the tools to express herself more clearly. She appreciates knowing more about leads and other genres. This helps me, as a teacher, know the importance of imparting to my students in my mini-lessons the techniques that enable writers to develop their craft of writing. Her comments also show me that Elana is developing her unique voice as a poet.

As I look back over her writing, I see many clues to her developing voice. In her sixth grade journal she tries out writing a descriptive paragraph by using the five senses in a paragraph about lightning (Figure 1).

The choice of words and phrases like "collapsing," "quiver," and "raindrops booming on the windowsill" here is striking. I love the way Elana ends this short piece with the image of the fog on the window "massaged away"; such touches are the first sorties of a poet. Her sixth grade teacher told me that Elana lived in a world of imagination and was often moody in class. She loved to be the center of attention, but often she retreated into herself or into her journal. Her writing at this point was mainly superficial but it held many glimmers of something more to come. In her sixth grade book of memories, Elana writes of her fear at the beginning of school and of her need to be accepted. She experiments with rhyming couplets. She also included a piece on her dance recital, integrating more of the effect of the five senses in her writing (Figure 2).

Other selections include a prose piece on her pet cats and a poem about her secret place in the woods. Sixth grade for Elana was a time for experimentation. She was becoming more aware of the techniques in writing that helped her grow as a writer: she was writing more clearly and with more details. Her responses to questions on a writing survey revealed more insights than previously. In answer to the question "What do you like to write about?" she replied: "I like to write either poems or descriptive paragraphs about certain places." She stated that her favorite kinds of writing were poetry and fiction and that her favorite author was Shel Silverstein, "because he's so funny, he can make anyone laugh."

Seventh grade was a year of change for Elana. Her moodiness increased and she was often absent because of depression. She argued frequently with her teacher and peers. Her writing increased in volume during this year and included many pieces about boys and about the personal problems she was having. I saw Elana use writing more and more to think about her personal issues; class writing

> When I remember my dance recital.
> I remember tasting my fear.
> I could hear my teacher
> yeling,"Alright!"Your doing it good! I
> could see the smiling,clapping and happy
> faces.
> I remember when I was a child yet I can
> still remember when I was dancing I
> felt a popping in my
> costume, particularly my big humungous
> lace that held my costume together, how
> much I hated that lace.
> Everyone started laughing and crying
> hard, and I remember I almost tasted
> my tears and the roses and cards they
> threw, but when I came off the stage
> I felt something new.
> I was no longer scared and no longer
> blue,but I was in the spotlight.

Figure 2: Elana's Book of Memories

was secondary for her, though she used class time to increase her proficiency in writing techniques and to explore topics in the outside world. She was lucky to be in a class that wrote every day. Her teacher also drafted Elana to work on the school newspaper, and Elana joined my after school writing group that year as well. This was when I became aware of Elana's many journals and personal poems. Slowly she began to trust me with some of her most personal work. In "Losing It" she wrote:

My thoughts are running wild in chaos and time is my only distraction. I have no more feeling in my heart, soul or mind. I have nothing more to feel. I'm losing the way I touch. That touch of me that makes people smile….

Elana was now developing her voice as a writer. She was learning to use writing as a way to create meaning out of the chaos inside her. Writing had become a personal journey for her.

Working on a special project (a content area writing project) on Inuit poetry with her class and the reading specialist, Elana also learned to see the world through other people's eyes. In Sun Song, the bright side of Elana appeared:

Sun Song

You are the sun,
The mighty father of nature.
Oh, sun, I shall cherish your
guiding moonlight that leads me
into the cold, barren Arctic
Nights.

You are the sun,
Colored by great beauty.
You are caressed with
exquisite shades of violet, blue
and pink.

You are the sun, the one and only sun.
Thank you for watching over your Inuit children,
And shower them with gifts of
Lichens and Fireweed.

You are the sun,
Filled with light but overflowing emptiness.

You are the sun.

This was also the year in which the school experimented more with portfolios and student writing evaluations as forms of assessment (see Appendix B). In a series of after school workshops, teachers decided that portfolios were a necessary step to keep track of students' work. Each teacher now had a crate and folders for storing student work. We tried to collect representative work, including narrative pieces, poetry, and student selected pieces with reflections. For her portfolio, Elana chose two very different poems, a poem of address to the moon and a four-page poem about racism. These poems reflect Elana's developing identity, one expressing her increasing concern with the social issues around her, the other showing a childlike delight in the natural world. She also included her piece "Losing It" and a narrative about a beautiful home.

In June Elana chose the poem "Let Me Stand In Peace" as her best piece of writing. She stated the following reasons:

I chose this piece of writing because I feel it's the best one I've done. I feel I let out what I had to say about my feelings about racism. I feel I called out to people who cared and maybe people who didn't. I think it's my best writing also because it's about an issue known in the world that a lot of chaos and madness is going because of it. I simply explained the ignorance of racism, and the ignorant people who are racist.

Elana is very clear about her choice. She is writing with a purpose and a passion. To me, as her writing teacher, I saw this poem as a turning point in Elana's developing voice. Not only does she write to solve her problems, she now sees that her writing can influence and move her audience. She writes with conviction:

Yeah, I'm somebody or am I not?
This world is crazy, beatings on the highways and in the parking lots.

Racism's got people wrapped around its hand,
From now to then when the whites got their land.

To the beginning of an awful story where no one wants to be friends,
When suddenly smiles and laughter come to an end.

Smiles into tears, handshakes into fists
Yeah, I know we all want to make it better, but when it all comes down to it, there's no one there to assist.

People wondering and hurting from all the disbelief,
While colored and uncolored walk with great grief.

Little kids losing playmates because of their different complexion,
But you're colored, too, so there's no need for your self-protection.

But it doesn't matter if you're French, Italian, Jewish, Puerto Rican, Dominican, or American.
I mean, you can be as American as apple pie and as Spanish as rice and beans, but

there's your face in trouble... AGAIN!

Her poem ends with these two stanzas that illustrate both the power of her convictions and the need to be heard even though she is "just a kid":

> *Remember, I'm just a kid so you better know where these words are coming from,*
> *I've always given acceptance to people, now don't you think you ought to give some?*
>
> *So keep remembering our ancestors of the late and the deceased,*
> *Let's learn from their wisdom and let me stand in peace.*

In a letter to me written in the summer after her eighth grade year, Elana reflected on her writing process:

> *Remember my poem "My Dreams?" You probably have a copy of it. Where sometimes I have these really bad nightmares of people being raped and killed. Sometimes my dreams inspire me to write those dark poems about race discrimination, violence, teen abortion, suicide and things. My dreams sometimes get me too far over the edge. I don't like having those dreams. But the good ones are always happy ones that end much too soon and just the opposite for the bad ones; they last too long.*

As a writer, Elana takes time to reflect on why she writes; in many ways, she has the wisdom of an adult. She helps me to appreciate the importance of such reflections, and I try to incorporate more student reflections in my current work with students. She has given me new insights into the minds of committed writers.

Elana differed from the others in our after school writing group in that she always had a writing project in mind. I saw her backpack full of writing folders and typed poems. As time went on, she began writing more personal narratives and love poems. Much of her writing concerned her search for identity and her place in her family:

> *In a town full of crime, disgust, and violence, there was a young girl stuck in the middle of everything. Her name is Elana. Elana Isabel Castillo. First name: after her abuelita, middle name after her Titi, Isabel, and of course, her last name was given by her father. You must of noticed that Castillo is a Spanish name. Puerto Rican as a matter of fact. Her ivory skin doesn't give anyone the slightest clue of her Spanish descent. Shoulder length tea brown hair blowing, sea blue-grayish eyes don't help them acknowledge that either.*
>
> *Elana's about five feet tall and stubby fingers and toes. Nails that always seem to grow but like her hopes and dreams, they always found a way to break. [Nails later appeared as a metaphor in a poem about lost hope.]*
>
> *Elana is very confused. Her heart is breaking. No matter how much super glue she'd put on her heart there was only one thing that would put it back together. Writing. Tough, her writing was tears, beautiful like a waterfall or the morning dew on grass but with a happy ending. Her poems warmed your heart and kept you confused but hurt. Hurt to know the truth you didn't even see....*

Elana's piece moves me; she makes me realize the importance of writing in her life. As teachers, we can never underestimate the power of writing to make a difference in adolescents' lives. I realized that we must provide the time in our curriculum for students to engage in writing that comes from their hearts and their experiences. As writing coordinator, I utilized the after school writing group as a way to fill this need. I also tried to provide more in-class time for writing about societal issues. As teachers of adolescents, we must let them know that we adults validate their struggle with both inner questions and societal issues. Even though these are convictions that I hold on to, I still struggle with the need to balance district and state curricular pressures with a strongly child-centered classroom. I look to my students to help me find the balance between state mandated assessments and a child-centered curriculum that provides students with opportunities for choice and initiative.

In eighth grade, Elana continued to write about themes of identity. She wrote more poems about boys, love, and friends (Figures 3 and 4). She wrote constantly in class, so much so that she often got in trouble with her classroom teacher because she wrote in her journal instead of doing class work. She seemed much happier this year, and much more flamboyant; her clothes and make-up were definitely those of an adolescent dying to grow up!

She also became much more of a reader. She would ask for recommendations from me and borrow books from our resource shelf. In an interview, she flatly stated: "You can't be a poet without reading. Reading and writing go all together." She read *The Homecoming* (Voigt, 1981), *Dicey's Song* (Voigt, 1982), and poetry by Langston Hughes and Maya Angelou, as well as excerpts from *I Know Why The Caged Bird Sings* (Angelou, 1969). I noticed in her written reflections on these authors' themes and styles that she had learned from Voigt to explore family problems in a complex fashion, and that from Angelou she had learned about poetic rhythm and, more importantly, that

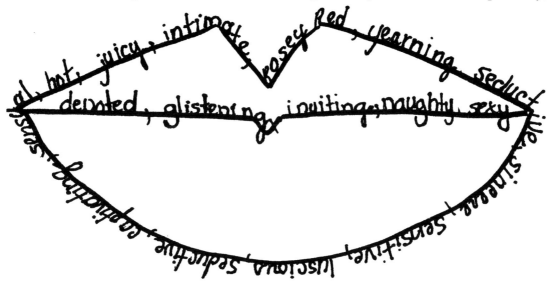

Figure 3: Elana's Poem on Lips

writing a personal memoir can help a writer move beyond her pain and into the beauty of words. I began also to see in Elana's writing new vocabulary choices that reflected the variety of her reading.

The following poem influenced by the French poet Rimbaud illustrates Elana's increasing delight with words:

A is red like the blood that bursts through my heart. Red like the fire that burns in your eyes. Red like the incandescent flow of passion.

E is yellow. Yellow like the rush of excitement. Smiles so bright and overpowering taking the sun's rays captive in its heat.

I is brown. Brown like the cappucino that spills over your eyelashes. Brown like the fuzzy covering that smothers our minds. Brown like this eagerness to taste this sweet and delicious color.

O is black. Black like the midnight sky standing alone and uncomforted. Like your souls' inner mystery full of secrets and hate. Black like a shadow stalking you at night, an imitation of what you are.

U is blue. Blue like the rolling collages of my eyes. The selfishness which lies beneath my heart. Blue like the ink I write with, a creation taken for granted and unacknowledged.

The lyrical language of this poem burst straight through my heart! I remember the day I first read it vividly because no sooner had the class read Rimbaud's poem than Elana was writing. She needed no further explanation or ideas for extended metaphors; she wrote her vowel poem in one draft with only minor revisions for word choice. I asked her how she did this and she replied, "I just got the ideas when you started reading. I can't wait until you finish because the ideas come too fast!" This experience confirmed for me that as writers we are all very individual in our processes; as writing

Figure 4: "An Actual, Affectionate Person"

teachers, we need to be sensitive to each students' needs and allow for flexibility in our methods. We need above all to become better observers.

This poem also illustrates Elana's sophisticated imagination and use of language and demonstrates that poets are influenced by the voices of other poets. Elana identified easily with the surrealistic reach of Rimbaud's words and integrated his concepts into her own experiences. Yolen (1994) asserts: "As a writer I am the empress of thieves…. I have pulled threads from magic tapestries to weave up my own new cloth" (pp. 702-703).

In the spring, Elana extended her lyrical writing to song writing. We were very fortunate to have a songwriter working with us, who worked with a small eighth grade seminar group for four sessions. Students brought lyrics and were asked to imagine what style of music they wanted to match to their words. Elana was always prepared with notebooks of lyrics. She knew her song "Crying Day by Day" could be set to "freestyle," which is a beat that incorporates salsa and ballad. Her song became a big hit in our school, and Elana found another avenue for her writing.

As part of a unit on realism, Elana wrote a memoir about her grandfather. She had written a similar piece earlier, but now she was ready to expand the paragraphs and add details. This brought back a lot of painful memories about alcoholism for her and she struggled with the revision process, trying in each draft to add richer details and to organize her thoughts more coherently. She also struggled with the tone of the piece, alternating between anger and love for her Papa. During conferences she kept insisting, "I can't do this. I hate writing stories. You know I'm a poet!"

I gently encouraged her: "But, Elana, you have the ideas all here. Just reorganize them to tell us how you feel about your grandfather. Sometimes it helps to write about the pain. Maybe you can learn something new from this piece. You can still be a poet here. Use your lyrical voice to tell your story."

```
        Papa had some nasty habits. He
preferred drinking rather than doing
something healthy. He drank vodka as if it
were flavored water. I'd have to say his
greatest addiction was to booze and to
television. While he laughed, he drank. Papa
really didn't have any hobbies. He just drank
and watched the Three Stooges. Day by day,
drink by drink, a new problem arose. Papa
changed while his addiction became harder to
break. Everyday was another episode of the
Three Stooges and another episode of
Papa's tantrums.
        I've always had mixed feelings about
Papa. Now that he's dead, I'm not sure
whether or not I should miss him, even
though I do. I'm not sure whether or not I
should hate him for ignoring Ma and favoring
Aunty.
        There are feelings of hate towards
him. I don't think I cry because he's
gone but because I never really knew or
had a chance to really know my Papa.
```

Figure 5: Elana's Piece about Her Grandfather

In each class she worked to organize her thoughts. In each class I gently *nudged* her (Calkins, 1991). When she finally finished, she breathed a sigh of relief. "It's done; I don't like it but it's better than it was!"

"Congratulations, Elana! I knew you could do it! I can't wait to read it!"

Her friends gathered around her. Roseanne said, "Oh, yeah, is that the piece about your grandfather. It makes me so sad. Let me see it."

Another friend, Yesenia, interjected, "Yeah, I remember you writing about him from last year. I want to see what you wrote this time. That part about the potatoes against the wall was gross."

Students at this stage were always eager to support each other's efforts. They knew how hard this piece had been for Elana. They wanted to applaud her, too. Reading her final draft, I could see that she had not only improved the organization of her paragraphs; she had captured the poignancy of her relationship with her Papa. This piece reminded me that sometimes we have to push even our best writers to places where they haven't been yet.

As a culminating project, our school published some of our students' poems as bookmarks, key chains and posters. Some of Elana's poems appeared and she continued to gain recognition from her peers. They clamored to have one of her key chains. The poem, "Nails" became one of the favorites:

Nails

My nails are like my dreams,
Weak and never seeming to grow.
They curve and split
Bend and flex
Until one day they grow and grow
But then they only find a way to
break.

Figure 6: Elana's Poem "Nails"

Elana continues to read and write. In a phone conversation after she started high school, she talked excitedly about reading *Raisin in the Sun* (Hansberry, 1994). She said:

> *Lorraine Hanesberry had an incredible life, didn't she? I mean, look how she writes. I want to read more about her life. I'm going to look for a biography about her. And Pearl Buck, we're reading about her, too...*

Elana talked about the books she was reading and how she had convinced her boyfriend to read *I Know Why the Caged Bird Sings* (Angelou, 1969). Reading books had become an integral part of her life. In a letter to me, she explained how she writes in her journal:

> *I'm using it as a diary. Not a **diary** diary. Umh, let me see if I can explain. Instead of writing about what happened in one day, I decided to use the journal and pick one incident of the day and write a poem about what happened that affected me the most. You get it? When my journal is filled I'll send it to you in the mail so you can read it. I'm pretty sure you'd like that. Wait, let me write you a page I wrote so you get the general idea. (Oh, and at the end of each poem, I write a little bit about why I wrote the poem so whoever reads it can get the idea of why.)*

> *Say it only once for I can*
> *hear*
> *What you say.*

> *Don't yell once more for I can*
> *see,*
> *what you mean.*

> *Do it only once for I can*
> *understand,*
> *Without being yelled at.*

> *Some people don't quite understand that children aren't as immature and naive as they think. Children, in my eyes, are more grownup because we must put up with the grownups when they act like children. So do you get the idea? I love my idea because it's so different from everyone else.*

ALYSSA: "It took three years for me to learn to write as well as I do.
When I first began writing, I couldn't even write one line that didn't seem plain.
Now each line I write has meaning and depth."

So begins Alyssa's evaluation of her growth in writing from grade six to grade eight. Like Elana, Alyssa came to view herself as a writer. She stated:

> *My best writing now is mostly poems, but I hope someday I will write a novel. Sometimes it takes me a while to choose a topic and a style of writing, but when I finally do, my writing just takes off. I often wonder how I can keep up with the pen gliding across the paper.*
>
> *I like to think of how lucky I am to have gotten the opportunity to become a great writer. When I think of how I've improved so far I can only begin to imagine where my writing will take me in the future.*

Alyssa is a methodical writer. A quiet student, she absorbs information and ideas and then takes time to reflect on them. At the beginning of grade six, she wrote the following in response to a survey: "I'm not too good at writing poetry, but I like to write poetry and essays." By grade eight her perspective had changed: "Poetry. That is what I write most."

As I look over Alyssa's portfolio, I notice a great change in the depth of her writing over three years. In grade six, her writing reflected an age of innocence and wonder at nature. The following is a typical poem:

> *Yesterday the sun was cold,*
> *but today the sun stands bold.*
> *Spring is coming!*
> *Spring is coming!*
> *Yesterday people wore coats.*
> *Today is warm enough for goats.*
> *Spring is coming!*
> *Spring is coming!*
> *Yesterday was a rotten day, but not today!*
> *Spring is coming!*
> *Spring is HERE!!!*

Here Alyssa plays with parallel structure and repeating lines. Her words, as she says, are "plain." Later poems show Alyssa practicing her use of metaphors:

> *Clouds are big cotton balls hanging in the sky.*
> *Clouds are big pictures painted on the sky.*
> *Clouds are big puffs of smoke coming from our father's pipe.*
> *Clouds are the carriers of rain and thunderstorms.*
> *Clouds are a sign of happiness throughout the world.*

Alyssa needs the assurance of form and practice with various techniques as she develops her writing voice.

In grade seven Alyssa joined my after school writing group. Here she began to blossom as a poet. Unlike Elana, Alyssa needed books or poems to read before she began to write. She needed models upon which to build a foundation for her writing. The following poem illustrates her reflective nature:

> *I like to be alone while reading a book drifting off to a place I've never been.*
> *I like to be alone while writing a poem letting my pencil glide along the paper.*
> *I like to be alone while thinking, just sitting deep in thought, thinking about many things,*

I like to be alone while staring at the stars dreaming about journeys through space.
I like to be alone in silence just to get to know myself better.

Alyssa confided that this after school group provided the quiet time she needed to write. It was too busy and noisy at home to write. This reminded me that urban students, in particular, need the quiet spaces schools can provide for writing. In these quiet spaces writers reflect on their lives, choose their topics, and grow through writing.

Alyssa also reminds me that writing often happens when one least expects it. One afternoon she was stuck for a topic but saw a frog puppet in our room. She wrote the following poem:

Hop! Hop! Hop!
That's what frogs do.
Why do frogs hop? I wonder, too.

Hop! Hop! Hop!
Frogs hop high,
Frogs hop low!

Hop! Hop! Hop!
Frogs hop far,
Frogs hop near!

Hop! Hop! Hop!
On the land, then in the air!
On the land, then in the air!

Hop! Hop! Hop!
Frogs hop here,
Frogs hop there!

Do frogs hop because of a special spring?
Do frogs hop because the ground is too hard for their soft, green feet?
Do frogs hop because gravity is not strong enough to keep them on the ground?
Or do frogs hop simply because it is fun?

Seventh graders often vacillate between their childlike world and their growing need for independence. They need the opportunity to explore the many facets of their personality before they can make significant gains in academic areas. As teachers, if we listen to our students, we can learn many lessons about how children develop as writers and thinkers. As I write these words I realize that many of these insights have become clear to me through closely observing my students.

Near the end of seventh grade Alyssa wrote this beautiful poem called "The Dreampath." She was inspired by a poem in the book *Rising Voices: The Writings of Young Native Americans* (1992):

When you are
lying lazily still
on your bed
on the sofa
or on the floor
not asleep
but caught
tight in a dream
this is called the
    Dreampath.

When you are

staring in wonder
out the window
into a picture
or at a wall
not studying it
but dreaming
letting thoughts
flow into your mind
this is called the
    Dreampath.

When you are
walking aimlessly
down the street
through the woods
or in your house
not just walking
but thinking about
everything around you
this is called the
    Dreampath.

Alyssa designed a poster for this poem, which was later published and copied for the school. Her poem inspired another student to illustrate her bilingual poem, "Green" in brilliant colors (Figure 7).

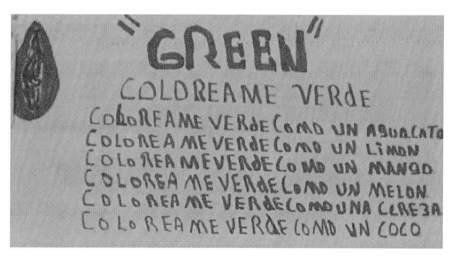

Figure 7: Simile Poem "Green/Coloréame verde"

In a later poem that same year, Alyssa declares herself a poet in no uncertain terms:

I am a tree poet sitting on the leaves studying the trees and when the leaves fall I fall with them writing poems about their beautiful colors.

I am a morning sky poet riding the wind writing poems about the birds flying by. My poems fly to earth with the birds of the morning sky.

I am a night sky poet swinging on a star writing poems about the shooting stars racing by. My poems race fast all over the universe on shooting stars…

Grade eight saw Alyssa expand her writing topics to those concerned with societal issues and memoir writing. As her favorite piece of writing in the eighth grade she chose the memoir she wrote about her third grade teacher. When asked what she liked to write about, she declared: "Everything, ranging from nature to issues like violence and crime."

I noticed too that her writing became stronger and more filled with conviction. Her voice speaks out against injustice as she sees it:

> *One voice is all you need to break the silence.*
> *One light is all you need to pierce the darkness.*
> *One flame is all you need to warm the cold.*
> *One is all it takes to really be bold.*
> *This voice should be your passport.*
> *This light should be your soul.*
> *And this flame should be your passion.*
> *Now use them to speak out and be bold.*

Here, we are reminded again that adolescents have a lot to say about what is going on in the world around them. Writing with conviction, they can put some order into the chaos that surrounds their daily lives.

TOM: "Now that I have developed into a writer, my goal is to use writing as a main source of my life. I intend to go to high school and keep up with my writing, and I hope to get to be an even better writer. And maybe someday writing will be the key to my success."

Tom wrote these words at the end of eighth grade, by which time he had learned to believe himself to be a writer. He became confident about his abilities and his voice. Tom, a very bright student, nevertheless walked a very thin line between appropriate and inappropriate behavior. Writing, for Tom, helped to channel his energies into a positive school arena; he gained recognition among his peers as a writer, not a fighter. I found that Tom's case was not unusual among my inner city students. Once they found a mechanism for expressing their feelings, their acting out behavior was minimized.

Tom also loved to read. From his earliest survey in sixth grade, he was able to identify authors whom he liked: Stephen King, Roald Dahl and Michael Crichton in seventh, and John Grisham in eighth grade. He always had a book with him in class, and he often engaged me in conversations about authors. He began to identify himself with these writers, and told me he wanted to become a novelist like Grisham. In fact, Tom's writing preference was definitely for fiction, and he had a natural gift for writing dialogue. I could see in his writing the influence of the writers he was reading. He was able to develop plot and character with ease *because of the books he was reading*. As his writing teacher, I tried to support these natural talents by encouraging writing that focused on his experiences and his observations of people in his life.

In sixth grade, Tom included his self-portrait and his portrait as an animal, both prose pieces, in his portfolio as his favorite pieces of writing. I noticed from the beginning that Tom enjoyed the process of revision; he worked hard on perfecting his leads and choosing the "right" words. The lead of his self-portrait reflects his early love of dialogue:

> *'He looks like a Tommy,' my mother said. 'Caroline, he looks like Roger!' said my grandmother. '"Wah! Wah!' cried the no named baby as my mother held me in her loving arms. My mother and my grandmother debated over a proper name for the new born baby, which was me at that time in the hospital.*

Tom also acknowledges his impulsiveness in this portrait:

> *I have an o.k. personality but sometimes if people get me mad I can get very mean. I have a tendency to speak before I think. I like attention and I'll be the first one to admit it. But*

when people take it too far I explode and when I explode, watch out! I have a very bad temper. But I am working on controlling it.

Tom is a very perceptive and honest writer. I often speak with students about honesty in their writing. I tell them from the beginning that they need to write the truth as they see it; they need to write for themselves, not for the teacher or for a grade. Adolescents need to hear this message many times. They need to be validated in their feelings and in their perceptions of the world around them.

It is interesting to note that Tom chose the tiger to research and then write about in his *persona* piece. Also notable in this opening paragraph is his choice of words: they reflect a growing vocabulary, the vocabulary of an avid reader:

As I observe my prey, I crouch low to see its movement. Then at the last moment, I leap from the jungle to kill it. I am a tiger, fierce and merciless. I am golden with long stripes that are blacker than night itself. My eyes are a dash brown with big, dark pupils. My teeth are huge and stained pink from the blood of all the prey I have terminated.

The third piece in Tom's sixth grade portfolio was a poem inspired by Byrd Baylor's book *I'm In Charge of Celebrations* (1986). In this poem, Tom celebrates Florida Day; this poem is noteworthy for its precise language and Tom's power of observation. It is obvious to me that Tom carries over his work in poetry to his descriptions in prose.

Florida Day is on June 30th. It is when I go to the sparkling shores of Florida to have the wildest time of the year. I start my day early with a cool shower and a cold breakfast. Then I am ready to go to the beach to see the awesome waves that beat the shore with tremendous force. The sun blazing with fury over every soul on the beach will send them home with a torturing burn. That's what I live for. The hot sun glistens on the crystal blue water. The sand is warm and smooth. The color is brown and gold. You can feel the warm breeze whirl through the beach.

Another poem written in sixth grade reflects Tom's experimentation with a poem of address:

Old yellow head, gleaming bright yellow, the sunshine of flowers running through the meadow.

Hey, moon flow, a milky white, you light up my path as I walk at night.

Old spiny back, hidden by trees, as I walk along you scrape my knees.

Hey, long back, so straight and firm, the largest of little plants. You share the woods with the birds.

Hey, white cup, so wild and free. We all step upon you but you spring up with glee.

In seventh grade Tom began to develop his style as a prose writer. His favorite piece of writing in seventh grade was a Halloween story that he wrote with a partner. He wrote the characters and plot and his partner wrote the setting. Here we see the influence of one of his favorite authors, Michael Crichton:

It was a dark and gloomy night in a street so spooky and dark that no one dared to be outside after seven. It was the kind of street that no one dared enter, not even black cats. The street was always slimy and creepy, not even a rat would live in one of the apartment holes. The street always looked dark, even when the sun was shining. No one dared pass by it for the street was haunted and when you pass by all you heard was moaning, creaky doors, breaking windows, groaning, and the rustling of trees. You would see shadows where there was nothing around. You could hear the squeaky little noises that mice make. [Tom's partner wrote this paragraph--great details!]

However, one day I was late going home. It was 6:45 and still daylight. The only shortcut home was Fifth Street. Now, as you know, no one would even get near the street but I had no choice. I started my way down the street and instantly my heart started pumping a mile a minute. It felt like people were looking at me from all angles. Then I thought I heard voices but I knew no one lived on this street.

I heard footsteps. I turned around and almost died. There before me stood a girl with no eyes; the sockets were sticking out of the two holes. She tried to talk but only moans came out. Then I noticed she had no tongue. I was very, very scared. I turned and started to run as fast as I could but the street never seemed to end. I looked at my watch and it was 7:00. I was late. But I kept running; the more I ran the longer the street got. Then I realized I was never getting out of this street. I stopped and she was the same girl I had seen before. She murmured something but this time I knew what she said. I was in another dimension. I thought about it and said, 'A dimension of what? Darkness? Fear? Mayhem? Or even Hell!'

Then an apparition appeared. He said, 'Neither of your guesses was right. This is a dimension of time.'

'Time!' I yelled. 'I don't have time.'

He said, 'Oh, yes, you do. Look at your watch.'

It was 6:45. I looked around and I was at the beginning of the street. The ghost said, 'I shall spare you from eternal hell. I was once a child, too, but time did not spare me!' I was saved! The ghost continued, 'Your courage may help this dwelling and all the dead will live again.'

'I hope so,' I said. Then, suddenly, the street seemed to lighten and I saw the little girl with no eyes playing. She was healthy and seeing. Then a man smiled at me. I smiled back. I made the dimension of time tick again.

Tom read this story over the intercom at the beginning of school one day, and his sense of drama while reading was impressive. He received more recognition from his peers and his teachers for his writing talent than for his earlier antics. I also sent this story out to various newspapers and magazines. As teachers, we need to find as many avenues for celebrating and publishing student writing as we can. I support their growth in writing by believing in them and spreading their voices throughout the school and beyond.

Near the end of seventh grade Tom became more aware of societal issues and began writing poems about issues important to him. The following poem was written at our annual Writing Conference:

Change

Try to change for the sake of others
Not only for you but for your many colored brothers.
White and black are just two colors.
Think of the world and of the many others.
People have tried but no one has succeeded to sort out the problems
that we are feeling.
I think a child can make a difference,
But we all need an adult's assistance.

Tom's eighth grade portfolio was marked by the variety of its contents, which were divided evenly into prose and poetry. In his self-evaluation, Tom wrote that his memoir of his grandmother was his favorite prose piece:

This particular piece of writing I like because I spent the most time I've ever spent on a

piece of writing. This piece helped me grow in my writing ability. It helped me to think more about my leads and conclusions. It's also my favorite because a lot of people gave it great compliments.

```
     My grandmother also likes to visit
Boston's North End. The smell of fried
dough, sweet-sour taste of lemon slush,
and the crispy texture of pizzele. It
excites her to walk down Hanover
Street and see all the Italian bakeries.
The sights, the sound, the feeling and
taste makes her feel like she was back
in the streets of Rome.
     My grandmother loves to cook and is
very good at it. Cooking for eight kids
you have to. She makes flavorful dishes
such as Steak San Marco and pork
chops and vinegar peppers. She has
always cooked well for me.
     Half Italian and half French, my
grandmother brags about being
"Italiano". Born and raised here
she doesn't like what has happened to
the city she used to know.
```

Figure 8: Tom's Memoir of His Grandmother

My favorite poem is "Should I Go?" [Figure 9]. This particular poem I like because it shows what happens to a kid who is asked to do something bad he'd never do on his own. It tells the facts and I think basing your writing on fact helps you get more ideas. It's catchy and honest at the same time. The writing is very coherent.

Tom demonstrates in these selections that he is aware of the elements of good writing and is aware of his growth in writing. By the eighth grade Tom had developed into a confident and articulate writer. In the following prose piece he shows both his gift for dialogue and his outrage at his treatment by police in an incident he experienced at a school dance. Here are a few excerpts:

During the night, I kept meeting eyes with a kid I didn't know. I did know his name was Jujo. He kept giving me dirty looks and I didn't like them, but I never said a thing. I wasn't the one who was going to start the trouble. As the night progressed, the dirty looks became dirty stares, and I started to bump into him more often. Then, finally, some kid came from behind and pushed me. If it had been Jujo, I swear I would have decked him then and there. But it wasn't Jujo. It was some white kid dressed in a purple silk suit, black suede shoes, the works. I asked him, 'What's your problem?'

He said bluntly, 'What's your problem? You think you're bad just because you're with your friends and because you're from over there? Well, you're not.' Just then my friend, Alex, came up to me and said, 'This kid got a problem?' I told him what happened. I guess we attracted some crowds. He had his friends and I had mine. I asked him if he had anything else to say.

He said, 'Ya.' Then he pointed to all of us and said, 'You all just better watch your back.'

Jay, one of my friends, said, 'No, we solve it here right now.'

We argued a little longer until one kid said to Jay, 'Shut up, you dumb white boy!'

Jay became too outraged to speak, so he put his fist to speak for him. In the next two seconds, the all too familiar sound of a closed fist hitting a face rang out. Before I knew it we were in a mini-melee....

And as quickly as the brawl started, it was broken up with the help of three police-

My friends tell me I should come along
go on a heart pounding ride
in someone else's car
should I do it?
should I not?
I could go on the roller coaster ride,
and face the possibilities of getting caught.
Or maybe I should not.
Restrain from the urge
To go on the ride.
And where will I end up?
What will I do?
Should I accept the challenge or no?
Should I stay home and wait for my
mom?
Wait for my dinner
Or go on the roller coaster ride
In someone else's car?

Figure 9: Tom's Poem "Should I Go?"

men. All of my friends and I were thrown up against lockers and one by one patted down thoroughly.

Then the oldest policeman asked me where we went to school. I wasn't going to lie so I said Braun School and his face lit up. He said,

'Well, well, well! Hey guys [to the other cops]. These guys are neighboring Braunencians. No wonder! Why do you have to come across town and start trouble with these nice kids? Do they come to your town and cause trouble over there?'

I said, 'No, Officer, because they're too scared.'

He asked me, 'Are you the leader of this little gang?'

'No, sir,' I said. 'We have no leaders. We're just a bunch of friends who came to a dance to dance.'

Then he said, 'Listen up. Enough wise cracks. This dance is for our kids only. We don't need you punks from over there coming across town and causing trouble.' I heard him *say racially insulting names under his breath.*

Then he gave us a lecture on how we should never step near this school again or face being arrested. After the lecture, the police officer escorted us out the door.

I know we shouldn't have been at the dance, but we shouldn't have been subject to a racial attack. Both police and kids contributed to bashing our town....

As Tom and I discussed the writing of this piece, I encouraged him to recall the incident in as much detail as possible. I encouraged him to recall the dialogue so that the characters would come alive for the reader. I did not judge Tom's behavior, although I could see that Tom could be headed for trouble if his energies were not directed in a positive way. I suggested to Tom that writing could help him sort out his anger and issues about prejudice and violence. As writing teachers, we need to support students' efforts in writing; our job is one of coaching, not judging. When we help students in this manner, we acknowledge the validity of their world. We build on their strengths as writers and observers. Tom made the following observations about his writing in the eighth grade:

In the 8th grade I think I have done my best work. I have almost perfected the art of bringing the reader in with captivating lead sentences, using the correct grammar, punctuation, etc. I also can say I have progressed in a way that I do not have to sit and think about what I have to write about or could write about. It just comes straight at me. I also can see that I can write more on my own than having to ask a teacher a question every five minutes. I have become somewhat independent. I can see I can write a story in which there are no questions to be asked after it is read. That means I put more detail in my stories than the years before.... In 8th grade I've begun to see I have a definite talent in writing and I intend to use it.

At the end of his self-evaluation, Tom thanked me for discovering his hidden talent. When we work as a community of writers, I deeply believe that we discover each other's hidden talents. Tom, Elana, and Alyssa are only three of many students who have helped me to develop my hidden talents as a writing teacher. They have helped me to see the beauty of their voices and have given me the passion to develop literacy lessons that will inspire them to read and write. Elana, Tom, and Alyssa have soared in their writing—indeed, writing has helped them survive the chaos in their world. The remaining chapters of this book recount the strategies that I have used to help my students' literacy take flight.

CHAPTER 4

Poetry of Identity: Building the Foundation of Prose Writing

The noise of thirty restless sixth graders greeted me early one fall morning. Their chairs scraped against the gritty floor as they bent to pick up papers and books. Sunlight played on the bare blue walls. Squeezing my way up the crowded aisles, armed with my bags of books and journals, followed by Marissa, who was carrying boxes of markers, I made my way to the front of the room where a lone table was waiting to be filled. I busily arranged my supplies as I waited for quiet. A crowd of eager kids asked, "Are those books for us? What's in that bag? Can we use the markers?"

"Yes, to all of those questions. First, though, we have to catch some quiet. When you're ready, I'll be ready to read to you." A small person with a soft voice, I've always found the most effective way to calm down a classroom is by standing quietly in front of the classroom with my books, waiting for the class to get settled. After a few times of saying, "I'm waiting for you," the class was ready to listen. The classroom teacher slipped silently into the back of the room.

I would have liked to rearrange the desks in a circle or anything but rows, but there was no room. Every square foot was filled with thirty-two desks and assorted materials. This would have to do. After all, I had a story to tell. Showing the class the cover of Mem Fox's lyrical book, *Wilfred Gordon McDonald Partridge* (1989) I began:

> *This is the story of an old person who has lost her memory. She tries hard to find it again with the help of warm eggs and singing shells. How many of you know some very old people? [Lots of hands.] While I read, try to remember them and also listen for how the author describes different people's views of memory. What helped Miss Nancy Alison Delacourt get back her memory?*

After reading the story, we talked about the author's beautiful language. I asked them how Wilfred Gordon brought Miss Nancy's memory back. Oliver, the classroom baseball star, offered: "When she held the warm egg she remembered the bird's nest in her aunt's garden." Andrea, who came from a big family, added: "I like the part about the puppet on strings. It helped her to remember her sister."

Malcolm, who was a newcomer to the class, joined in: "What about the shell? It helped her to remember the beach and her buttoned up boots." As students recalled these details I wrote them on the board. Then I began telling them the story about my Greek grandmother:

> *When I began writing poetry I wrote a lot of poems about my grandmother. She was very special to me because I grew up with her in a tenement in Boston almost like the ones here in your city. When I began to write about my Greek 'yaya,' the smell of mint invaded my thoughts, the sounds of bargaining for lettuce in the Haymarket seeped into my ears; I could even see her gray sweater and black gardening shoes. My memory was filled with these sensory details, and by writing I was able to pull them back out. Listen to this poem about the Haymarket where my grandmother and I used to shop. Can you imagine this place?*

> *I wander between the narrow streets*
> *remembering the endless crates and vegetables broken*
> *push-carts heaped and steaming, crowded*
> *a garden of flowers and colored lights hanging*

cornering my senses, drinking my fill
I silently sip the lemon slush

Forgotten for a moment is the gray slush
beneath my leather boots--the streets
are alive with smells, sweetbreads fill
my senses, the raw hot dogs are broken
divided among the slabs of beef hanging
from the ceiling, sentinels amid the crowds

The tenement stores have a pulse, peeling, broken
lovers shout out windows, children precariously hanging
out of windows, laughing, eating slush…

Do you see how I used all my senses to recall the Haymarket's noises and smells? Can
you taste the lemon of the slush? Writers use the five senses to make their writing come
alive. They want the reader to share their experiences.

While giving out blank journals, I encouraged my students to draw upon their storehouse of memories to write about a special person or a special place in their lives. "Weave into your poems your native languages. If your grandmother speaks Spanish, use Spanish words in your poems. Try to be as specific as you can."

Writing the following form on the board was a way to help students who might be stuck for a way to begin. Beginning is often the hardest part of writing a poem, and "How do I begin?" is the question I am asked most. In working with second language writers, I have found that a form that allows for flexibility ensures success for students at all ability levels; they always have the option of inventing their own form. I also believe that this simple form liberates students to concentrating on forming an image rather than worrying about the arrangement of lines:

When I Remember My Special Person
I see
I hear
I smell
I taste
I touch

The teacher and I circulated around the room, gently helping students to explore their memories. Speaking to Emily, I learned about her grandmother in Guatemala. I commented, "Emily, I would love to meet your grandmother. Can you describe her for me? Does she have a special name for you? My grandmother always called me "Sugar" because I was so sweet. What does your *abuela* (grandmother) call you?"

"She calls me *chiquita*," Emily replied. "It means 'little one' in Spanish."

"That's a great sounding word, Emily. Maybe you can use that word in your poem today."

I wanted Emily to know that using Spanish in her poem would help to bring her grandmother to life. Using heritage languages in poems makes the poem authentic to both the reader and the writer. It validates our identities. Emily later shared this poem with her class (Figure 10).

I love this poem by Emily. Although it contains few specific details, the ones that are present are lovely: the spring-smelling perfume, the sound of *chiquita*. The poem has a gentle feel for me. In writing poetry with second language learners, I praise all their efforts; I work little on revision at this stage. I want them to begin to feel confident about writing. As they become more proficient, we add more details; in future lessons, we might open our journals and find a poem such as this and revise it with detailed images in mind or start again with another person.

As the class went on, we heard about Elizabeth's old house in Missouri, where "policemen have

When I think of my
Grandmother?

I see her cooking for us.

I hear her singing and
calling me chicita in the
morning.

I taste her baked cakes.

I touch her soft delicate
skin whe I hug her.

I smell her perfume that smells
like spring.

I see my Grandmother
in her house in Guatemala.

Figure 10: Emily's Poem about Her Grandmother

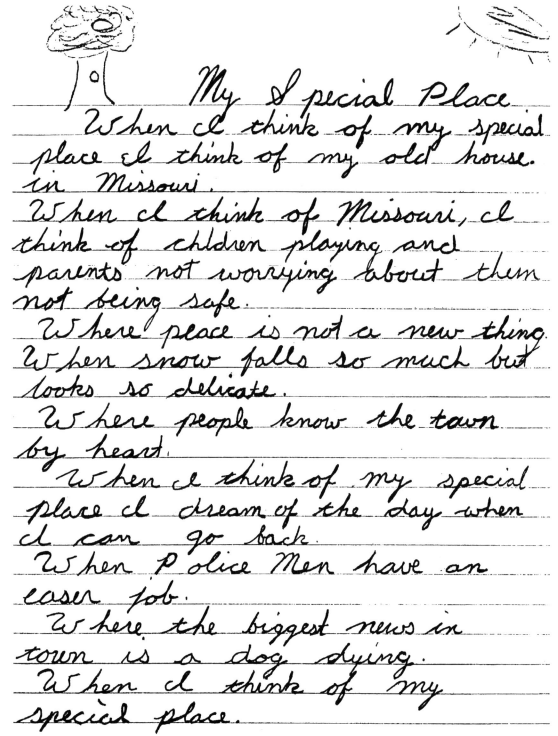

My Special Place

When I think of my special
place I think of my old house.
in Missouri.
When I think of Missouri, I
think of children playing and
parents not worrying about them
not being safe.
Where peace is not a new thing.
When snow falls so much but
looks so delicate.
Where people know the town
by heart.
When I think of my special
place I dream of the day when
I can go back.
When Police Men have an
easier job.
Where the biggest news in
town is a dog dying.
When I think of my
special place.

Figure 11: Elizabeth's Poem about Missouri

an easier job and the biggest news in town is a dog dying" (Figure 11).

We also heard about Daphne's grandma and tasted the vegetables that she grew in her garden. As the students continued to share their poems, we began to realize how unique we all are. We began to see the power of words to transform our classroom into a space filled with memories. At the end of the class, which was usually about fifty minutes, I urged students to put their final draft poems on unlined or lined paper; they could surround their poems with beautiful borders using the markers I would leave with them. The classroom teacher agreed to help with last minute edits for spelling and display their poems in a writer's corner. I hoped that the walls would soon be covered with beautiful poems.

Digging Deeper for Details

For the next several weeks in writing workshop I worked with students to add more details to their writing. Like Lucy Calkins (1991), I am always trying to "nudge" writers forward. I especially want them to know that what they have to say is important and that I am interested in getting to know them through their writing. I shared insights from authors, often beginning class by sharing quotes from books like Donald Murray's *Shoptalk* (1990) or Pamela Lloyd's *How Writers Write* (1987). I told the students:

> *I'm interested in what authors have to say. As a poet, I can learn a lot about writing by hearing what other authors have to say. I was just reading a book called* Long Quiet Highway *by Natalie Goldberg. Goldberg says that having a sense of place is a very affirming and steadying influence on a writer and that if you learn to love one place, then you are more aware of other places.*
>
> *Remember last week when we wrote about special people and places. I wonder if today you could reach back into your memory for a very special place, a place that you like to go to when you want to be alone and quiet. Maybe you already started a poem like this, but forgot to add enough detail to make it come alive for us. Listen to how Nikki Giovanni uses the five senses in her poem "knoxville, tennessee" to make us feel that we are at the summer barbecue in Knoxville. She makes our mouths water with descriptions of fresh corn and buttermilk and homemade ice cream!*
>
> *Did you see how the poet used the five senses in her poem to bring us to Tennessee? She was specific. She named the exact foods that she loved like okra and greens and barbecue. We can almost be tickled by her barefoot toes! Today as you write stretch yourselves to add more specific details in your poem. Bring us to your special place.*

I circulated around the room and conferenced with students, urging them to be more specific in their descriptions: "Mark, when you go to Turbury Pond, what animals do you see in the water? What kind of barbecue does your family eat?"

Next to Mark I noticed that Irene was writing about her closet. "Irene, I used to love to hide in my closet, too. I couldn't budge in there because it was so filled with heavy wool coats. What's your closet like?" These kinds of questions not only show students my interest in their writing, but also serve as a mini-conference, providing students with the scaffolding that they need to continue their writing by adding more details.

As I moved around the room, students were less hesitant about writing. They often asked their friends to read their poems; if students finished in five minutes and couldn't think of anything else to write, I would help them by asking more questions about the place they were trying to describe. I emphasized to them that I needed them to tell me all about their places because I hadn't been to them myself.

Leaving time to read aloud the poems that students have written is a crucial step in writing poetry together. Poems need to be read aloud so that everyone can hear the music of the words. This also gives me an opportunity to give kids instant feedback on their poems and share with the class my favorite images or sounds. If students are hesitant about sharing, I might begin by sharing one of my own poems:

> *I love the pine woods*
> *with its pine needles smelling*
> *of golden earth*
> *with its chickadees chirping*

dee-dee-dee-dee and
flitting from branch to branch.
I love the quiet of the place
I hear its stillness
in the music of the wind,
brushing the leaves
of the forest floor.
I feel the smoothness of
the ladyslippers beneath my fingers.
I love the quiet of my special place.

Irene volunteered next. Her poem about the closet brought lots of smiles and knowing nods among her classmates (Figure 12).

We all laughed over Irene's line that described how lazy she was. She made us all remember the

My Special Please Is...

My special please is my bedroom closet. My closet is special to be because when I'm upset with tears dripping down my red face, I go into the closet. It felt like I was going into a cheer up home. I lay on my pink fluffy blanket and lay my teary face on my soft pink pellow that feels like a pile of feathers laying on the floor. I accidently tasted my tears. It tasted kind of sour like a sour lollipop. I just lay there in tell I fall a sleep. I heard my mother calling me saying "Joey come and eat supper". I was too lazy to get up and I said to my self, "If I'm any lazier I'll slip into a coma". So I just got up and went to sleep.

Figure 12: Irene's Poem about Her Closet

times when we felt like sleeping the day away!

Sometimes, friends read the poems of their friends if they were reluctant readers. In this way all our voices could be heard. Little by little, writing was bringing us closer together as a class. We were learning to trust each other's voices.

PERSONA: Hiding Behind a Mask

People of all cultures have used *personae* in poetry for centuries. When we use a *persona* in poetry, we mean that we write in another voice, be it animal, vegetable, or human. *Persona* is a safe way for adolescents to speak of their true feelings from behind the mask of another voice; they can speak about their emotions without fear of ridicule from their peers. For seventh graders, who seem particularly peer conscious, this provides another avenue for expression.

As I help children develop their poetic voices, I use their knowledge of writing with the five senses to develop "personae." One fall I brought into a particularly difficult seventh grade class a heaping basket of fruits and vegetables that represented the fall harvest. Many of the students in this class were Title One students and many came from dysfunctional homes. They had begun to show some glimmers of interest in writing over the previous weeks as they wrote about their grandmothers or friends. I hoped that bringing in concrete objects would help them write with greater detail and that writing in *personae* would give them the freedom that comes from hiding behind a mask. They crowded around the basket, pointing out the limes and lemons that had also been included to represent fruits from the Caribbean, but the gourds, eggplants, and squashes mystified them!

I began by introducing the notion of *persona* as a poetic technique:

"What does the word persona mean? Come on, you know this word; it's the same word in Spanish."

"*Person*," Nellie shouted out." I knew that." Nellie was often in trouble and twirled her hair in class and had to be prodded to write with each new assignment. The previous week she had written a moving poem about her grandmother and I had high hopes for her.

"You're right, Nellie. *Persona* does mean "person," and when we write in the voices of other things, like animals or vegetables, we are using a technique called *persona*. As I read this poem to you about mushrooms by the poet Sylvia Plath, think how the poet became a mushroom. In her poem she describes the texture of mushrooms, how they might move, and where they live. She provides very specific descriptions using the words "we" and "us" to make the mushrooms become persons. Think about what vegetable you might like to become."

After reading the poem, I commented on the author's use of metaphor, simile, and personification. I added that poets, like scientists, are astute observers of nature and choose strong nouns and verbs to express their thoughts. I also showed many pictures of mushrooms to illustrate how mushrooms are like "tables," "shelves," "nudgers," and "shovers."

Next we discussed the various vegetables and fruits in the basket. We looked at the onion and as I peeled its various layers, I commented on its thin, papery outside texture. I asked, "Do these layers protect the onions' feelings? What secrets are inside me? How is my inside different from my outside? Can you always judge a book by its cover?" As I asked these kinds of questions, I was asking students to "become" the vegetable, to give these inanimate objects feelings, personality, and names.

I held up the eggplant. No one knew its name, but they loved its smooth purple skin. Passing around the eggplant, I said, "Do you think I belong to a royal family because of my elegant purple robe? Are my cousins princesses?"

Of peppers, the classroom teacher declared, "Look at my variety! I belong to a multi-colored family!" And of the banana, Josie declared, "We have those in Puerto Rico. They have the shape of a moon."

English language learners at all levels of English proficiency can be engaged with these kinds

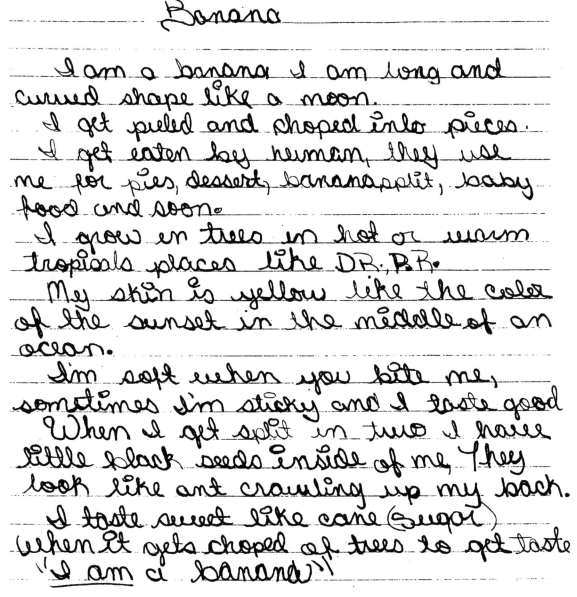

Banana

I am a banana I am long and curved shape like a moon.

I get peeled and choped into pieces.

I get eaten by human, they use me for pies, dessert, banana split, baby food and soon.

I grow in trees in hot or warm tropicals places like DR., P.R.

My skin is yellow like the color of the sunset in the middle of an ocean.

I'm soft when you bite me, sometimes I'm sticky and I taste good

When I get split in two I have little black seeds inside of me, They look like ant crawling up my back.

I taste sweet like cane (sugar) when it gets choped of trees to get taste "I am a banana"

Figure 13: Lisette's Poem in the Persona of a Banana

of questions and discussions. Often, these kids are given stacks of worksheets without really being required to think; while playing with metaphor and personification, and using their powers of observation, however, these seventh graders were pushing their higher order thinking skills and expanding their vocabularies. They were also planting the seeds of good writing.

The teacher and I helped the students in their planning by drawing a web on the board that incorporated the elements of our discussions: outside texture and color, inside texture and color, family members, environment, personality, children, friends, clothes. They then chose a vegetable from the basket for which they would write a *persona* poem. I encouraged them to smell, touch, shake, and see the vegetable from every angle. Poets above all are keen observers, and they sometimes discover words through their fingers.

We were lucky to have three teachers in this class—the classroom teacher, the Chapter I teacher, and myself. We all circulated and helped students find the words to describe their vegetables. We praised their efforts, no matter how small. Willie, who rarely wrote, chose the sweet potato because his grandmother often cooked them. He wrote:

I am a sweet potato.
I am bumpy and long.
People use me to eat, to fill their stomachs with joy.
I smell sweet and taste delicious.
They put me in a microwave and I heat up and I am like the sun.

And Lisette, who was often absent, had no trouble choosing the banana, which was familiar to her (Figure 13).

I was proud of her use of personification when she talked about her skin and of her comparison of the inside seeds to ants crawling up her back. I asked Lisette to read her poem to the class so others could feel proud, too. Poets develop in small spurts, but each time they try something new, they are adding to the variety of the techniques they can use in their writing. We all need to recognize each other's accomplishments, no matter how small. Writing is about taking risks. We can help adolescents take risks in the safe environment of their classrooms, hiding behind the masks of fruits and vegetables. We can become anything; that's the magic of poetry!

Writing about Animals: Developing the Powers of Observation

The seventh grade special needs inclusion teacher burst into my office one day to tell me how much her students benefited from all the art that we did along with the poetry:

'They really need this multi-sensory approach. Some of my kids still can't write without help. They need so much help. We're studying the Arctic environment in science. Some of the kids are reading Dogsong *by Gary Paulsen [1987]. Are there any other ways to make connections? Do you have any books or pictures? Any ideas?'*

'What about writing in the voice of animals? This usually grabs the attention of even the most reluctant writers. I have loads of pictures from Audubon and National Geographic magazines. I could share what I know about Inuit poetry. Much of their poetry was written in the voice of animals. What do you think? I'll bring whatever picture books I can find and come in tomorrow. Would that work?'

She replied, 'Sure, we'll try anything!'

Teachers came to me more often now with requests for help. A community of trust was beginning to grow up around writing. We had begun to build up our resources in the Writing Center, and every day teachers would drop by and ask for help or materials. Classes would be planned very much like this one, a quick conversation, a suggestion or two. I knew most of the kids in this class from my work with them in sixth grade: Dana, Benny, and Julio, who still needed lots of help, along with Elana, Lea, Vanessa, Kathy, and Cynthia, a core group of very talented writers. Before I went into class, I dropped off the magazines and books that I had: beautiful picture books like *Arctic Memories* by Normee Ekoomiak (1992), *Eskimo Boy: Life in an Inupiak Eskimo Village* by Russ Kendall (1991), and *Arctic Hunter* by Diane Hoyt-Goldsmith (1992). I am a firm believer in using picture books with middle school students, and I knew that these books would attract lots of attention. Knowing that non-fiction is a great way to hook readers, I also knew that the pictures would help writers find the sensory detail that they would need to write their poems.

When I entered the classroom, which was the last room at the far end of the courtyard, the kids were busily looking at the pictures, deciding which animal they might like to be. The walls were covered with kids' writing and artwork; writing was clearly important in this room. The teachers had even devised a plan to pair the less able writers with more talented ones, which seemed to work very well. Having the students engage in the background work of searching through the pictures was a great help to me in getting everyone ready for writing class. Besides my inevitable straw bags filled with markers and paper, I also had Inuit art prints and calendars, which I had collected in Montreal.

I am a giant of the ice pack.
I am a polar bear and that's a fact.
I live in the cold, frigid and treeless tundra of Alaska.
I have strong teeth and sharp claws.
My heavy white coat keeps me warm.
It is pure white like the glistening snow, and the
puffy white clouds floating in the sky very calm.
I weigh more than a ton.
I am extravagant and diligent.
I wander neither than migrate.
I keep my fierce eyes secured for a seal each day.
Even though my hearing is poor, my eyes are sharp
And I can smell a dead whale twenty miles away.

I see many ptarmigans fly over the sunset.
I hear the call of the wild.
I smell my prey already dead.
I touch the cold Tundra all the miles!
I taste the salt water very smoothly.
I love the Arctic Tundra.
It is my home and my habitat.
And no one will destroy it and that's a fact!

Figure 14: Vanessa's Persona Poem as a Polar Bear

After hanging up a few prints and posters behind me, I began by sharing my personal interests with them: "Sometimes writing grows from things that we have seen in books or places we've been. As a poet, I'm very interested in the poetry of Native American cultures. So, one summer I went to Montreal to study more about Inuit/Eskimo art, because I was working with another class on their study about the Arctic, just like you are. I found a book called *I Breathe a New Song* (Lewis, 1971), which had many poems written by Eskimos in it. I learned a lot about how these people view the world by reading their poetry. One thing I learned was that they respect animals, and before they kill a seal they say a prayer to it. Sometimes these prayers are written in the voice of the animal itself. This shows even greater respect. I thought today we could try writing one of these poems because I know you've been studying about the Arctic and all its beautiful animals. What can you tell me about the animals you've found?"

Benny said, "I know the seal is a great diver and it can live under the ice."

Julio added, "Yeah, and it's skin is oily, too. Yuck!"

I asked Lea, a quiet Chinese girl, what she had found out. A wonderful writer, she had to be prodded to contribute orally. "I found out that the polar bear eats salmon and has huge black claws. Its hearing is poor but its eyes are sharp."

"You know what else?" I asked, "The polar bear is called The Great White One by the Inuit people because of its huge size. When you're writing in the voice of your animal today, think what

They call me the Great White one.
Strong and fierce I can be, I am big
I hunt with my young, but I know danger
is amoung us
I am not afraid
I move slowly without a sound
across the tundra combing the snow, with my black claws
I find salmon for my young, they eat and I protect
I see danger toward us, with my small eyes.
I will not fight, I run with my young,
with the world around us, with the cold,
with the tundra
I am the Great White One, I am!

Figure 15: Lea's Persona Poem as a Polar Bear

name you could call yourself. Think about your characteristics and how you move. Use what you learned in science class to write your persona poem today. Do you have enemies? What do you eat? What might your personality be like? Choose an animal that you know something about or would like to become."

I then read the poem "Desert Tortoise" by Byrd Baylor because of the beauty of its language and pointed out the use of the first person pronouns, *I* and *my*, in the poem. "Notice how the tortoise calls itself 'the old one' in this poem. Notice how it describes its shell: 'My shell still shows the tooth marks where a wildcat thought he had me long ago….' In your poems today, write in the first person as you describe yourself. Remember, the Inuit believe you are powerful when you become the animal. I believe we are powerful when we write. Let's see what we can create today."

48

As the teachers and I conferenced with students, we pointed out pictures that showed the large tusks of the walrus, caribou running through the tundra, and seals diving for fish. In other words, we pointed out a variety of details that our students might be able to use in their poems. Dana was having a hard time that day; she just didn't want to do anything and couldn't decide on any animal. We gave her a few magazines and markers and hoped that she might start by drawing. Sometimes we found it best to leave Dana alone with her thoughts. By the end of the class she might try again.

Vanessa, a Cambodian student, wanted to get her details exactly right. She spent the entire period reading about polar bears and taking notes: "I live in the cold, frigid, and treeless tundra of Alaska.... I weigh more than a ton.... I wander rather than migrate...." For her, finding the right descriptive words to describe the polar bear was paramount (Figure 14).

Lea, on the other hand, wove the facts she found into more poetic terms, digging deeper into the persona of the poem. Her poem draws us into the essence of life as a mother polar bear (Figure 15).

For each of these students, the process of writing this poem was very different; as writing teachers, we need to be sensitive to such differences. We all grow at different rates and see the world from unique perspectives. To me, the value of poetry is its ability to let us see the world in extraordinary ways. Through the voices of *personae,* adolescents begin to both appreciate multiple perspectives and speak about their feelings from behind the mask of another person. Later, when Vanessa wrote a magic word poem in the voice of an Inuit, she expressed the need of many adolescents to have their own views heard (Figure 16). Writing is about finding one's innermost voices.

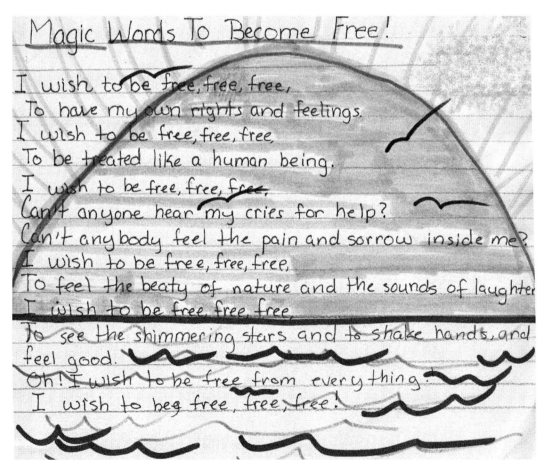

Figure 16: Vanessa's Magic Word Poem in the Voice of an Inuit

The Sky in My Hands: Accelerating Academic English through the Writing Process

ODES: Addressing Our Universe

Driving to work after a snowstorm one crisp morning as I was, I was blinded by the sun glistening off the snow-covered trees. Their whiteness against the blue sky was almost too much for me! After reading Pablo Neruda's odes the day before, I was inspired to write an ode to winter. There was just no better way to express my feelings about winter! Armed with my poem and calendar pictures of wintry snow scenes, I thought about seizing this moment with my sixth grade writing class. I hoped to convey not only the technique of writing an ode but the idea that poets are moved by the beauty around them; sometimes poems are born this way.

When I arrived at school, I bustled around my office looking for black construction paper and white paint. We would paint snow scenes after we wrote today. The peeling walls could definitely benefit from our acts of beauty. The classroom teacher had begun taking some after school writing classes with me, and was beginning to feel more comfortable about risking new ideas; the class was also starting to loosen up and was writing more often and with more clarity.

As I entered the classroom with several helpers, the other kids saw the trays of paint and ex-claimed, "Are we painting today? Did you see the snow piled up outside? I bet we're writing about snow today!"

Seizing moments was beginning to feel natural to these sixth graders. This was a real sign of progress in their growth as writers. They were becoming poets in their outlook towards nature. I began class with my story about discovering odes by reading Neruda's poems, odes that he had writ-ten about lemons, socks, shoes, the moon—just about everything! I explained that odes are poems of address in which the poet can address inanimate objects as though they were people. We could tell them how much we loved them or even tell them we hated them. I shared my poem from the previous day:

Winter,
yesterday you came
with frost on my window
ice off the marsh.
You came with cold precision
and short days. Now,
the daylight splinters the sun
into shards of icicles.
Your cold breath
shuts me in the house
by the fire,
content to drink hot chocolate
and read novels about Mexico.
Your rough hands dry my skin,
enveloping me
in a coat of Arctic air.

Winter,
You surprise me
each year with your harshness
and avalanche of snow.
Your frozen fingers
drape trees and bushes
in white filigree.
Your harsh voice
drives my cats

inside
under the blankets.
Winter,
you are the Emperor
of ice.
I shiver in your grasp.

"Do you see how I spoke to winter in my poem as though it were a person? Do you see how I describe the frost and the ice off the marsh? Living in the city, you might have different perceptions of snow. Think about what snow sounds like on the streets? What do you do when it snows? "

Ramon called out, "I like to throw snowballs! I like it when we have a snow day and I can bumper ski with my friends."

"Bumper ski?" I asked "What's that? I've never heard of it."

Jason added, "That's when you grab onto car or truck bumpers and slide down the street with them. It's fun!" Jason was always getting into trouble and had a troubled home life. I knew for him this kind of danger was the best part of snow. How different from my perceptions of the world!

"Well, you could write about bumper skiing! I'd love to hear more about it. In your poems, try also to give winter personal qualities. What did I mean when I said winter had 'cold breath?'"

"The wind?"

"Yes, exactly, see how smart you are! But saying wind is kind of ordinary. By saying breath, I can make my poem more personal. See how extraordinary you can make your poems today by giving winter names for its hands and its coldness. Later we can put our final drafts on beautiful paintings in white and black."

I placed my poem on an overhead so they could see the form that their ode might take. I pointed out the use of the second person pronoun *you* in this type of poem because in an ode we address something or someone. I also pointed out the use of personification and metaphors in the poem to make winter come alive. This kind of modeling and then further pointing out the structure of the poem gives second language writers the tools they need to be successful in writing their own poems. Some asked to look at pictures for more ideas; others needed help finding the metaphors to fit their images. As writing teachers, we are there as guides and coaches, and, yes often as cheerleaders. We helped students to translate the beauty outside their windows into words.

Yolanda, who had just come back from a month visiting her relatives in Columbia, expressed her dislike for the cold, although she did like to play in the snow; I urged her to express her feelings in her poem and to describe winter the way she experienced it. What did she notice about the snow outside her house? Her final poem (Figure 17) entrances me with its images of winter sitting on her doorstep and its fingers freezing her ears!

Like Yolanda, I loved to play in the snow; she brought back my childhood memories. In seizing moments through poetry, we can all learn to play in the snow again. We can reach back into our childlike innocence and revel in the simple pleasures of life. For adolescents, this reaching back is just as natural as moving forward. I believe that writing poetry provides a time for our students to equalize the pushes and pulls of growing up in our fast-paced society. On that brilliantly cold day in Yolanda's class we slowed down enough to take a moment to share the beauty around us. We made a connection to the earth on which we live.

BRAVADO: Hiding Beneath Exteriors

In my experience, eighth graders are typically much more aware of the world around them than their younger peers. Those who grow up in the city also experience first-hand the real fears of violence in their neighborhoods. Many have witnessed the deaths of friends in gang shootings. Some worry about the environment and the increasing pollution they see around them. Most also experience conflicts with parents or friends. Their world can be a frightening place. Writing poetry, I

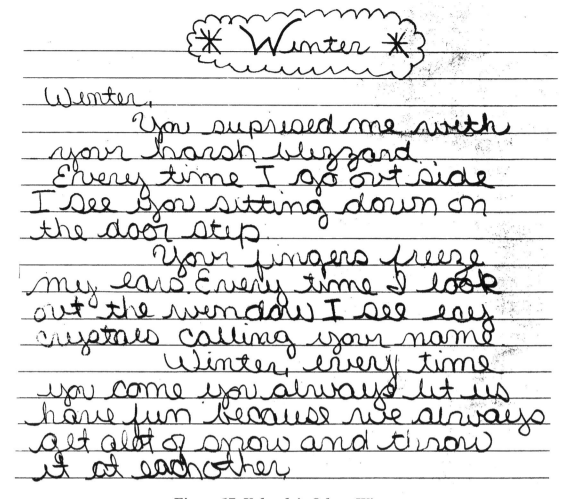

Figure 17: Yolanda's Ode to Winter

believe, is a vehicle for expressing these fears; by writing we can make meaning out of the chaos around us.

Bravado is a poetic technique that lets the poet hide his or her fears behind the mask of bravery. Rhyme is often used to give the poem a playful quality. For adolescents, *bravado* can become a way to express their innermost anxieties without fear of being ridiculed by peers and without fear of judgment. As a writing teacher, these poems help me to get to know my students better.

One eighth grade class was particularly out-spoken; the students had views about everything and weren't a bit shy about talking about them. They could be quite disruptive, so early on I took advantage of their "enthusiasm" by channeling their energies into writing. There were many good writers in this class—kids I had known for two years, kids who loved poetry.

While they were reading *I Know Why the Caged Bird Sings* (Angelou, 1969), I seized the opportunity to introduce Maya Angelou's poetry. Sharing a personal experience, I began:

"About ten years ago, I had the opportunity to hear Maya Angelou speak at a conference in Boston. That day changed my life. The audience was swept away by her presence; as you can tell from your reading, Angelou is a strong person. And when she reads her poetry she puts her whole body behind her voice, making you believe that words can have the power to change your life. She told the audience: 'You may encounter many defeats, but you must not be defeated.' Her words changed me that day; I read all her books. Not only did her words help me to get through difficult times, she helped me to believe in my own strength. Sometimes poetry has that kind of power—that's why I believe in it so much. Sometimes we all have things that we are afraid of; writing can help us figure out why.

"Look in the packet of poems that your teacher and I gave you and find her poem *Life Doesn't Frighten Me At All*. She uses a poetic technique called 'bravado.' That means that she is putting on a brave face to the world; she might be really frightened, but by writing about her fears in an almost playful way, she is putting her problems behind her. She juxtaposes reality with fantasy. First she mentions 'shadows on the walls' and other scary things; then in the next stanza she talks about Mother Goose and nursery rhymes.

I pointed out some of the other elements in this poem, such as a rhyme scheme, a repeating line, and a line that reads like a child's chant ("Step on the rack, break my mother's back"). Such observations help students to begin thinking about techniques that they might employ in their own poems.

"Today, in your writing, think about what fears you have. When I wrote a poem like this I wrote about worrying about my teenage daughters driving into Boston to dance in clubs. What things bother you?"

Rosangela, who I often teased with the name *la gerente* because she loved to manage everyone's business, interjected, "Fighting with my friends—we always seem to have problems now—it's bad."

"Boys, too, they're always a problem," Yesenia added.

"Gunshots at night, that's what scares me," Andre said.

As the kids talked they found out that they had a lot of the same fears. They could easily identify with poems about this topic, and they could also see that they were not alone. Too often we feel alone with our problems; poetry helps us not only to find meaning but also to realize that we all share the ups and downs of life.

I suggested that they could "borrow" Angelou's technique by writing short lines and repeating her line "life doesn't frighten me at all." By apprenticing ourselves to poets, we can try on other voices as we discover our own. Andre, who is very sensitive, wrote:

> *Blood lost in war*
> *Violence emerging more.*
> *Life doesn't frighten me at all.*
> *Knowing I will die,*
> *Famine causing cries.*
> *Life doesn't frighten me at all.*
> *Peace nowhere to be found*
> *Guns and knives all around*
> *They don't frighten me at all.*
> *Peace becoming extinct*
> *Fearing countries will never link.*
> *That doesn't frighten me at all.*
> *Kids being abused*
> *People not knowing who to accuse.*
> *I just smile*
> *They go wild.*
> *Life doesn't frighten me at all.*

What strikes me most about Andre's poem is his concern about what's going on around him. I have found that middle school adolescents have a lot to say about society's problems; writing poetry is a way for them to convey their feelings effectively and with passion. I believe that we adults must listen to the voices of our children, for they are the voices of the future. I want to give my students hope that they can make their voices heard and can make a difference in their lives through writing.

Speaking Out: Writing to Change the World

In the spring of that same year, I attended a conference sponsored by Facing History and Ourselves, where I heard high school students from New York City speak about the interviews they were conducting with the homeless and with victims of abuse and gang violence. A choir from a Boston school sang about the power of dreams. Thinking about my own students, I knew that their writing had been at its most powerful when they had the chance to speak out against racism and violence.

Wanting to share with the eighth graders the vision of these New York and Boston students, I entered Andre's class the next day filled with great hope and carrying a new book.

"Where were you yesterday?" Rosangela asked. "We missed you!"

"Your outfit's fresh, " Elana called out."I want that choker!"

"Okay, okay," I laughed. Let's settle down. Take out your journals. Let me tell you about where I was."

As kids were settling in, I told them about the young people whom I had heard at the conference.

"These kids from New York and Boston interviewed kids all across America about issues of racism and violence. They published a book called *Voices from the Future* [1993]. It contains interviews and poems. Listen while I read one of these poems."

As I read one of the poems, called "Land of Diminishing Dreams," about drugs and war, students listened thoughtfully and shook their heads in agreement. Many began writing while I was reading, filled with the urgency of the moment. I simply asked them to respond to these readings by writing poems that would convince others to stop and listen. Previously, Rosangela had told me that her cousin had been killed in a shoot-out, Gabriel had written about a cousin who had died in a drug deal gone bad, and Carlos had bragged about getting in trouble for stealing cars. These students knew pain first-hand; they were also beginning to realize that they had the future in their hands, that they had control over their choices. Writing, for adolescents, is a way of taking control, of making positive choices; through poetry they can, as Rosangela said, "write with what's on my head and not what's on my mind." They can write about the urgency of moments.

The students wrote that day quickly and powerfully. They couldn't wait to share what they had written. They were writing with purpose and conviction. Gabriel, who was usually hesitant to share his writing, volunteered to read his poem:

> *When will we wake up?*
> *Pop! Pop! Pop!*
> *Now there goes the body drop.*
> *Now here come the cops.*
> *Now tell me when will this ever stop?*
> *Brothers and sisters killing each other*
> *Trying to rob and steal from one another.*
> *The war must stop.*
> *We are the future or if not we won't have one*
> *If we don't stop the killing.*

The class cheered Gabriel, and then others read their poems, one after the other. They had something to say, urgently. Hong, another quiet student, read:

> *Have we forgotten the past when our children can play out on the streets freely?*
>
> *Have we forgotten the corruption of Evil as our peace and harmony fall into the hands of a history book to be written as just words?*
>
> *Have we forgotten a time when we didn't have to lock our doors and hide in corners because of fear?*
>
> *What have we forgotten?*

These are the moments that I cherish most in my teaching—hearing kids speak with conviction in their writing. This class taught me to trust my instincts and to trust adolescents' voices. For me, poetry is the vehicle that liberates students to speak from their hearts. They find the words to move us to tears, laughter, and wonder. They find the words with which to speak to the world:

One Voice

One voice is all you need to break the silence.
One light is all you need to pierce the darkness.
One flame is all you need to warm the cold.
One is all it takes to really be bold.
This voice should be your passport.
This light should be your soul.
And this flame should be your passion.
Now use them to speak out and be bold.

    Alyssa

Poems in Two Voices

Writing poems in two voices is another very successful strategy in working with students in the middle grades. This technique also provides an excellent opportunity for students to write a poem collaboratively. My use of this technique in the classroom has been inspired by Paul Fleischman's books *Joyful Noise* (1988) and *I Am Phoenix* (1985). I begin by introducing some of Fleischman's poems on transparencies; I divide the class in half so that each group has a "voice" to read. I also demonstrate that the line printed in the middle is meant for both voices to read in unison. I then show a poem that I wrote about hair spray when my daughters' hair spray bottles began to overwhelm the bathroom. I recounted how I read the ingredients of one bottle and found that the words had a rhythm that I could turn into a poem. Whenever possible, I want to demonstrate to students my process as a poet; I also want them to know how I came to write a certain poem and how I am influenced by the experiences and events in my life. I want, especially, to demystify the writing process.

      Hair Spray

New

                                                      improved

20% stronger

                                                   sculpting foam

                    With conditioners

fast drying formula

                                              made from organic

Australian flower

                    Extract

for scrunching

                                              spring

and styling.
Aromatherapy

                                                Aroma-ology

cherry

                                                almond bark

pure flower

                                                plant essences

                    Rejuvenating
                    Conditioner
                    For hair.

I discuss with students how poems in two voices lend themselves to expressing two opinions by different people or things (personae); they also lend themselves to the expression of conflicting voices within ourselves. We brainstorm possible topics, from the mundane (dialogues between sock and shoe, basketball and hoop, or sun and moon) to issues such as prejudice, politics, and the environment. Students then pair up and I suggest to them that each partner assume the role of one of the "voices" as they write. The following poem by Brian, an eighth grader, illustrates the diversity of topics that can be explored:

Hockey

The puck is dropped

You crosscheck the center

You're shorthanded

You're jeopardizing the game

Hockey
They score--it's 1-0

But you tie it up 1-1

Second period, you play them tight

It's still a tie

Hockey
Third period, you slash a man in the leg

You're in trouble.

Up against the best power play in the league

They score--it's 2-1.

Hockey
High sticking, cross-checking, slashing

What for, two minutes in the box.

You're down 2-1, in the final game

And then you get a penalty

Hockey

Until he wrote this poem, Brian was a fairly disinterested writer. I knew that he loved hockey and I encouraged him to write about the excitement of playing a game using all the sports jargon that he knew; this particular form was also perfect for showing the movement of the puck on the ice. This became one of Brian's favorite pieces of writing.

In my experience, eighth graders, who are usually very shy about reading their poems aloud, readily volunteer to share these poems with the class. Poems in two voices can thus become a natural vehicle for celebrating students' writing.

Even though I continually stress to students the importance of hearing their poems—hearing the music they have created with words—middle school students are often inhibited by peer pressure. I am always looking for strategies that will enable students to read their poems dramatically. Additionally, exchanging their poems and reading them anonymously at the beginning of each class allows students' voices to be heard. I have seen adolescents' faces light up as their poems are read, and looks of recognition are flashed across the room.

Extending Identity: The Unifying Theme

As students begin to discover themselves through writing, they find their voices transformed, like ice, into a new melting or configuration of words. Through poetry, they look at themselves through the lens of metaphor and simile. Exploring identity in a variety of forms is yet another way for adolescents to grow through writing. I may begin this exploration by reading poems such as Eloise Greenfield's poem "By Myself," which is replete with metaphor and a sense of beauty in being brown. Another poem I like to read aloud is Julio Noboa, Jr.'s poem, "Identity," which contains the following stanza:

> *I'd rather smell of musty, green stench*
> *than of sweet, fragrant lilac,*
> *If I could be a tall, ugly weed.*
>   *(Noboa, Jr., 1987, p. 148)*

When I asked students in my eighth grade class what the metaphors in this stanza meant, Emily answered, "It means it is better to be yourself than to be part of a gang." I deliberately choose poems that suggest this theme because today's adolescents are faced with tremendous peer pressure, and resisting takes the strength of one's convictions. Writing is a way of giving students an opportunity to develop this inner strength.

Another one of my favorite poems to share is "I Know that Feeling," by the Native American poet Simon Ortiz (1974), in which an American Indian shouts out his identity from the top of a steel girder while working on a skyscraper. When I ask students what the "Feeling" of the title is, they invariably answer "pride." Since I want to promote in my students a feeling of pride in their roots and their cultures, I search for poems like this one that sing with pride.

After looking at a few poems like this, we discuss the use of metaphor to represent our uniqueness. For example, if we have a violent temper or are impetuous, what things in nature could we use as comparisons? Julio answers, "Volcano;" Lisa suggests, "Tornado." Other students build upon these initial responses and suggest earthquake, hurricane, or rainstorm. To illustrate other character traits we brainstorm using a web. Then I share on the overhead the following poem, written by one of my seventh grade students many years ago:

Who Am I?

I am a small blade of grass in an open field.
I am an oak tree reaching for the sky.
I can be raised up like a soufflé, but then flattened if someone yells.
I am a sparkling ballroom, but sometimes a dusty old attic.
I am like a new shoe--it takes time before I fall apart.
I am like a '57 Chevy. I may not be in style, but I last long.
I am like a cozy fire--warm and friendly.
I bring happiness to those who need cheering up.
I can do amazing things if given a chance!

I point out this poem's strong metaphors and the writer's technique of beginning many lines with "I am," which shows the positive spirit of an adolescent who is both sensitive and strong. We discuss how fragile our feelings are at this age, and I emphasize that we can all do amazing things if we are given a chance; we can especially do amazing things in writing if we take risks and write with honesty.

The poet Ruth Whitman inspired me to further explore my identity through her poem written in the form of a questionnaire. The following is my own poetic spoof on a questionnaire, with my answers written in metaphor:

Questionnaire

Describe your early education.
At three, I learned the warmth of a black coal stove in my grandmother's kitchen.
I watched her nimble fingers knead the dough.
Time measured in a measuring cup.

What is your permanent address?
A deserted beach where the seagulls screech

A cathedral step among the crowded tenements
A university library among the books.

Are you married?
Joined with rings
Separated into reality
Searching for reality
Searching for independence.

Describe a crucial event in your life.
At twenty-eight, I gave birth to a delicate daughter
I learned the jubilance of volcanoes, the fragility of small fingers,
 the fuzzy softness of hair and skin
I dreamed ageless mother dreams.

List your awards and honors.
Daughter
Wife
Mother
Teacher
Woman.

I discuss with students how my answers represent various aspects of myself and how, unlike conventional answers to such questions, they take account of the fact that we are constantly changing. In writing poems on this model, I ask students to choose the most significant aspects of their lives—crucial events that have changed them forever—and to name as awards those intangibles of which we are most proud, with the last named being the most important. Though this assignment is complex, I have found that eighth graders generally enjoy experimenting with this poetic form. In particular, for students who are already comfortable using metaphor in poetry, this form can challenge them with its novelty.

Rodrigo wrote the following poem in response to this assignment:

Describe your education.
School has not showed me all I need to know.
My ability to write poetry has showed me the power of the mind.
I've learned through writing how powerful words could be.
In my life I don't have many highs but just as many lows.

What is your permanent address?
At the gymnasium playing basketball
At the park playing baseball or football
Out in a quiet place where silence is dominant.

Describe a crucial event in your life.
September 17, 1987 my motherlike grandmother died
June, 1992 my grandfathers died
November of 1988, 1989 my little brothers were born
December 8, 1991 my smallest brother was born.

Awards or honors.
MVP of NYC City Champs
Member of city champs and Massachusetts runner's up
Won the Youth Leadership Award in June
Honor roll first semester.

Rodrigo's poem showed me again the power of words. As middle school teachers, we often look out on a sea of impassive and seemingly bored faces. When we ourselves speak with passion and conviction about poetry, our students, in turn, speak with the same passion. They begin to see new possibilities, new genres to explore. I also discovered something else: by sharing a slice of my life with my students, I made them more willing to share their lives with me.

Name poems are another effective way of celebrating both our uniqueness and our identity. In this context I like to read aloud the lyrical vignette "My Name" from *The House On Mango Street* by Sandra Cisneros (1989). I ask students to think about their names as I read other models. Do they like their names? Do their names suit them? Do they know what their names mean or whom they were named for? Do their names have sounds that remind them of something else or of other words? Other poems that I read include "How A Girl Got Her Chinese Name," by Nellie Wong (1993) and *Nathaniel's Rap* by Eloise Greenfield (1989).

Yesika, an eighth grader, wrote the following name poem:

> *Mi nombre fue creado por mi mamá y mi papá.*
> *Es una mezcla del español y el inglés.*
> *Mi hermana me llama Jejika.*
> *Mi hermano me llama Lilia.*
> *Pero, ¡hey! los dos dicen lo mismo.*
> *Dicen que mi nombre suena como una pelota.*
> *Muévelo pa' quí, muévelo pa' lla,*
> *salta por aquí, salta por allá*
> *Yésika también suena como un yoyo.*
> *Brinca, salta, muévelo también.*
> *Yésika es la fé.*
> *Mi nombre siempre será el mismo.*

Before Yesika began this poem, she asked me if she could write her poem in Spanish; when I responded with a resounding "Yes!", she was thrilled. Even though Yesika is in a "mainstream" class, her native language is part of her identity; she told me that she still thinks in Spanish. I think that it is crucial for teachers to understand that as students travel in the world between two languages, they need the opportunity to express themselves in their native language. Such opportunities are important in their transition to "thinking" in English and writing beautifully in their new language. I asked Yesika to write a translation of her poem so that her classmates who do not speak Spanish could appreciate her beautiful poem. In this way, I was validating both Yesika's identity and her writing. She wrote the following translation:

> *My name was thought up by my mom and dad.*
> *It's a combination of Spanish and English.*
> *My sister calls me Jejika.*
> *My brother calls me Lilia.*
> *But, hey, they both seem the same.*
> *They say my name sounds like a basketball,*
> *Jump up, jump up, and get down.*
> *Yesika also sounds like a yo-yo*
> *Move up and down, Jump up and down.*
> *Yesika is the name.*
> *My name will always be the same.*

I have found that students seem to intuitively know the aspects of their name that reflect their personality. Yesika's poem is filled with "j/y" sounds and words that have syllables and meanings that dance and move to reflect her "on the go" personality. Likewise, Tara, a seventh grader, played with the syllables and connections in her name:

> *My name is like a cheerleader cheering Ta-ra-ra-ra!*
> *My name is like a star in the sky that you wish upon.*
> *My name is like a cake, instead of Sara Lee, it's Tara Lee.*
> *My name feels just right; it's not too soft and it's not too rough.*
> *My name is short, it's not too long.*
> *My name is perfect for me in every way!*

Carlos, an eighth grader who loved to rap, wrote the following:

> *This is a story about C.P.*
> *A kid who rocks the mike throughout the country.*
> *He's really cool and he likes to chill.*
> *And watching him play ball is a real big thrill.*
> *And behind his muscle bound body is a hidden treat*
> *Cause on the ball court he could never be beat.*
> *He is really bad and really fresh.*
> *He's Carlos P. and he's in the flesh.*

Carlos had no problem sharing this poem with his peers! He is self-confident and proud of himself. I urge students to celebrate themselves in these poems; this is no time for modesty! We can be whatever we want to be, whatever we create. Most of all, I want my students to experience the sheer pleasure of playing around with sounds and images in these poems. A playfulness with words is the necessary ingredient in all good writing. I want students to experience the same joy in words that I feel, a feeling that is definitely contagious.

I recently discovered the book *i live in music* by Ntozake Shange (1993), with paintings by Romaire Bearden. As I read this work, I realized that it could inspire students to write about the great passions of their lives—whatever it is they "live in." Based on Shange's model, my students have written poems on art, dance, comics, soccer, acting, and many other topics. The possibilities are endless!

I believe in general that the possibilities for teaching writing are endless. I am never satisfied to teach a mini-lesson the same way twice, because I am constantly discovering new books, new authors, and new ways of exploring identity. There are no prescriptive ways of teaching—that's what makes teaching an art form. I often think of teaching as poetry in motion. As I discover exciting pieces of literature, as I experiment with writing, as I interact with my students, I am constantly discovering myriad approaches that will help both my students and myself to grow in literacy.

The "Who Am I?" poems, the "name poems," and the *i live in* poems are all possible beginning explorations of identity. When students become comfortable with writing about themselves, I introduce the idea of a monologue poem. A monologue is a narrative poem that is written as though we were having a dialogue with ourselves about issues that are on our minds. This kind of poem allows students a lot of freedom in both form and topic; it also validates adolescents' concerns about friends, dating, parents, school, peer pressure, drugs, or other societal issues.

I have found Mel Glenn's books of poetry, *Class Dismissed!* (1982) and *Class Dismissed II* (1986), to be very effective as starting points for discussion. These books present short poems as dramatic monologues spoken by teenagers; they create pictures of the diverse hopes, dreams, and fears that characterize the population of any middle or high school. After reading and discussing several of these poems, I ask students to write about what problems or concerns they might have on their mind that day. I have found these poems, such as the following, to be among the most moving student works that I have seen:

There's a problem.
I'm a smart kid but I used to mess around a lot.
And now when I try to stop everybody wants me to keep causing trouble.
I wanna be popular with all the other kids, but now getting into trouble is
hurting me a lot.
And if I keep it up it could mean my hockey career.
You see my father is gonna take me off the team if I keep getting in trouble.
So, which way should I go, good or bad?
     Brian

Get To Know Me!!
Why is it that when I think that I've finally found someone true to a friendship,
they end up showing me their true colors?
If you're my friend
Be my friend.
If you're my foe
At least get to know me first!
Don't judge me by the way I look or by the way I dress
By the way I talk or by the way I walk
Judge me for the person I am!
And if you don't like what you hear or what you see
I guess it's better that you
Just stay away from me.
     Paula

These poems give a hint of the diversity of feelings within a single classroom. This class had many problems with students getting along with each other. However, it also contained some of the most gifted writers in the eighth grade. I always tried to capitalize on their strong writing voices to highlight some of the issues with which they were struggling. This proved to be very effective in helping students see each other from different perspectives. Their writing also emphasized the positive aspects of their behavior, and provided models for those students who would rather be disruptive than creative. As I read these poems aloud, anonymously, I observed nods of recognition and glimmers of acceptance among the writers' peers.

When I speak with my students years later they often remind me that poetry has touched their lives in many ways. Two such encounters come to my mind, both of which happened in unexpected places. Recently, I was staying at Pinkham Notch Camp in the White Mountains, getting ready to climb my next 4000-foot peak, when two young women entered the room wearing jackets from Concord-Carlisle High School, the school my daughters attended. I asked them if they knew my youngest daughter, Jennifer, and Katy responded that she was in my daughter's class. Then, out of the clear blue, she said to me, "You know, I still remember when you visited our sixth grade class when we were studying Inuits, and you read us their poetry, and then we wrote our own poetry. I really liked that!" I couldn't have been more surprised since at the time, I would never have guessed my impact. Seven years later, Katy still remembers the power of words! A few years ago, one of my oldest daughter's acquaintances, whom we met at a meeting for international students, confided to her that she was going to major in English in college because she loved the poetry that I brought into her classes in the sixth and seventh grades.

These stories tell me that as writing teachers we never know how literature will affect students' lives. I do know, however, that if we bring our passion for books and writing into our classrooms, our students cannot help but be affected. Words can, indeed, change our lives.

The next chapter describes how poetry becomes the basis for writing an autobiography in sixth grade.

CHAPTER 5

Developing Our Voices: Inside Sixth Grade— Poetry, the Foundation of Descriptive Writing and Response to Literature

Hunting for Metaphors

At a New England Reading Association Conference in October of 1993, the author Kathryn Lasky urged her audience to treat language like a beautiful antique. What a great metaphor, I thought to myself. Language is priceless, valuable, and delicate. When I write poetry, I often think of the fragility of my words. How could this reverence for words be developed with my sixth graders? Why not have the students search through anthologies for poems that use startling metaphors? Why not go on a metaphor hunt?

The next day, I began collecting poetry anthologies: *The Random House Book of Poetry* (Prelutsky, 2000), *Sing A Song of Popcorn* (White, Moore, and De Regniers, 1988), *Animals, Animals* (Carle, 1989), *A Fire In My Hands* (Soto, 1991), *The Place My Words Are Looking For* (Janeczko, 1990), and *Cool Salsa* (Carlson, 1994). My arms full of these, I needed the help of several students to carry the construction paper, glue, scissors, old magazines, and markers. "What are we doing today?" they asked excitedly as we headed for the classroom.

"It's a surprise," I teased.

Charlena guessed, "We're going to find poems in these books. What else could it be? My arms are aching. This better be good!"

"You're going to love this, I promise."

As we entered the room, we were greeted by the usual hubbub of noise and greetings. This class never approached anything with a neutral stance: they either loved what we did or hated it! We emptied our supplies onto the front table. The excitement was mounting as they saw the variety of things before them. I held up Kathryn Lasky's new book, *Think Like an Eagle* (1992), and began my story:

> *Yesterday I met a fabulous author: Kathryn Lasky. She's most famous for her non-fiction books, but she has the heart of a poet, just like you do. When she said that language was a beautiful antique, I knew for sure that she was really a poet. Let's listen carefully to her words, and see if we can hear what she means to think like an eagle.*

The kids listened raptly as I read. Beginning classes by reading stories aloud never failed to calm down these sixth graders. They were curious and hungry for words. How many of them had been read to when they were younger, I wondered? Stopping about halfway through, I asked, "How does the wildlife photographer in this story think like an eagle? What does that mean, do you think?"

Oliver quickly answered, "Well, when he hides to shoot his pictures, he has to be quiet. He has to wait a long time until the eagle comes so he can take a picture. Boy, he must be tired!"

Marissa interjected, "See, he's like an eagle because he has to get inside the mind of the eagle. He has to be a good hunter, too."

"Do you think that we could go hunting today, too, right inside this classroom?"

"No, we'd need guns!" Julio shouted. Everyone cracked up!

"Well, Julio, all we need today are our minds and books, because we're going on a metaphor hunt. Work with a partner to find a favorite poem, one that compares something to something else without using the words 'like' or 'as.' When you find it, write it in your journal. Later, we'll put these poems on posters with illustrations."

Going up and down the aisles, I dropped books on students' desks amid cries of "No, I want that one!"

"Don't worry about it, you can always exchange books. The important thing is to find a poem! Remember, hunt your poem down like eagles!"

As the kids worked with their partners through collaborative inquiry, their teacher and I answered the repeated question "Is this a good one?" with assurances and encouragement. They found wonderful poems that day, poems like "Cumulus Clouds" by Sheryl Nelms, "Cardinal" by Barbara Esbensen, and "What Is Black?" by Mary O'Neill. They had fun with words and the joy of discovery along with learning that partners can be a great help to each other.

The next day, we put these poems on posters with illustrations. I had copied some of their favorites so that they could cut out words and make a collage if they wanted. They could even look in the magazines for words to add to their illustrations.

The following week, upon entering the room, I was surprised to see the walls covered with the students' finished posters. "Wow, your room looks great! You guys are really talented!"

"Yeah, we know it," shouted Tom. There was nothing shy about Tom. Tom was always pushing the envelope of acceptable behavior, but he was an avid reader and a talented writer. He was very charming when he wanted to be. I couldn't give up on him. Knowing Tom loved music, I came prepared that day.

"Is everyone ready for some music today? Listen to the lyrics of *The Wind Song* by John Denver and Joe Henry. These authors probably knew a lot about metaphors and Native American poetry."

Musical hooks became a natural link for me between lyrics and poetry—even reluctant writers were drawn in by the beauty of the music. Music also helped us to relax and appreciate the musicality of words. This particular song is an excellent example of the use of metaphor in lyrics. Each stanza begins with another name for wind, like "The wind is the whisper of our mother the earth." The kids listened carefully for the different names for wind and tried to write as many as they could in their journals. When the song was over, I asked:

"What names for wind did you hear?"

The room waved in a sea of hands. Emily replied, "'A goddess who first learned to fly.'"

Gisella answered, "'A twister of anger and warning.'"

And others: "'A weaver of darkness.'" "'The bringer of dawn.'"

"You are great listeners! Today, in your writing, try to write a poem filled with metaphors. Choose something from nature and write as many different names for it as you can. Try using personification; that is, if the wind blows, we can say it dances. When you are finished we can put these poems on beautiful paper. Let's see what you can do today."

Circulating and conferencing with students, I observed the sophistication of their images. One student named the wind "a dance partner waltzing with the grass and trees." Adam called a dream, "a love song keeping you in its trance, the mother of thought, a multi-colored renewal of life." Each poem I read was better than the next. This confirmed my belief that children have an emotional connection to the earth and to image making. Maria wrote the following poem:

> *A rainbow is a paintbox full of colors.*
> *A rainbow is the color of our skin.*
> *A rainbow is the future of my dreams.*
> *A rainbow is the mother of the rain.*
> *A rainbow is a paintbox's twin.*

Maria was a quiet, sensitive student who worked diligently on her assignments but hardly ever contributed to class discussions. Yet writing poetry came naturally for her: it was as if she were talking to her best friend.

Journal Response to Reading

On a cold February morning, I entered a sixth grade classroom with two books: *Tar Beach* by Faith Ringgold (1996) and *Owl Moon* by Jane Yolen (1987). The kids' faces were all pink with the cold and the room was almost as chilly as the air outside. I began:

Let's see if we can warm ourselves up by transporting ourselves to other worlds through books. I'm going to read two books this morning, Tar Beach *and* Owl Moon. *One takes place in the summer in New York City, the other in the winter in the country. They're both stories about families. As I read, think what these books remind you of in your own lives. When we read, we are often reminded of similar experiences or of people we know. This is called interacting with the text* [Rosenblatt, 1985]. *Good readers make a book their own by identifying with the characters, the setting, or the experience. When I read a book, I escape into another world and reflect on what personal feelings I have towards the characters. Sometimes I write my feelings in a journal. I wrote this response* [Figure 18] *after reading* Crossing to Safety *by Wallace Stegner* [1987].*

This is a beautiful story about family and friendship. In my response I identified with the writer's need to get away and write down his thoughts and I reflected on my wish that I had friends like the ones in the story.

After listening to Tar Beach *and* Owl Moon, *please respond in your journals with the experiences that either book reminds you of. See how you connect to these books.*

Silence enveloped us all as I read. We were transported to our unique worlds. After writing we shared our responses, the variety of which amazed me. Daphne responded to *Owl Moon* with memories of early morning sled rides with her father (Figure 19).

Gisella responded to *Tar Beach* with several above ground experiences (Figure 20). Notice how Daphne responded to a character, whereas Gisella responded to the city scene. *Owl Moon* reminded Malcolm about walking with his father and their dog in the woods in New Hampshire. Emily thought about Guatemala and how when the lights went out she would take out a flashlight: "I felt like an owl in the woods, because I could see in the dark."

These responses demonstrate the uniqueness of our personal reactions to literature. When we respond to books, we are, as Nancie Atwell (1990) so aptly put it, having conversations around the dining room table. Have you ever talked to a friend about a book and asked about the main idea or the sequence of events, or do you talk instead about what moved you in the book? The way we respond to books is the way children respond, too. Often, they need modeling or suggestions to stimulate thoughtful responses, since they are so used to merely summarizing plots. This experience convinced me that I needed to incorporate more exercises of this kind into my teaching.

A few weeks later I read to this same class *Letting Swift River Go* by Jane Yolen (1995). This book, about the flooding of a town to build the Quabbin Reservoir in western Massachusetts, moved me to tears and reminded me of the time my neighborhood in Boston was destroyed to make room for something new. Beginning by sharing my response, I asked students to think about a time in their lives when they might have lost something important to them or a time when they had to move because of outside circumstances. My students' lives were filled with stories about loss—loss of family, moving to a new country and climate, loss of fathers or mothers, and so on. I wondered how this story would affect them: how would they connect?

As we shared our responses, we heard stories about houses in the neighborhood being burned down and about going back to the Dominican Republic and finding everything different. Harry responded as follows:

The book reminds me of a clubhouse I once owned. This old man didn't like kids. I built the clubhouse in the yard, but he broke it down. I built one more, nice and sturdy, and I put a lock on it so he could not break it. I had the clubhouse for six months. Then I had to

Response after reading chapter 6
Crossing to Safety

Sometimes I long for friendships as ideal as the ones that the couples Sarah & Larry had with Sid & Charity. They had so much in common — a love of writing, music, & the outdoors. Plus, they were so willing to share their wealth, both personal and material with each other. Their thoughts traveled along the same wave length. Possibly, there's only one such friendship in a lifetime, or maybe it's just fate — being in the right place at the right moment. I've always wondered about that question.

I can identify especially with Larry, the writer as he yearns to write every day and wishes for an escape into Florence, Italy where he can devote himself for a year to writing. What a luxury!

I can't wait to see what happens next, especially how the couples continue to grow with each other.

Figure 18: My Response after Reading Crossing to Safety by Wallace Stegner

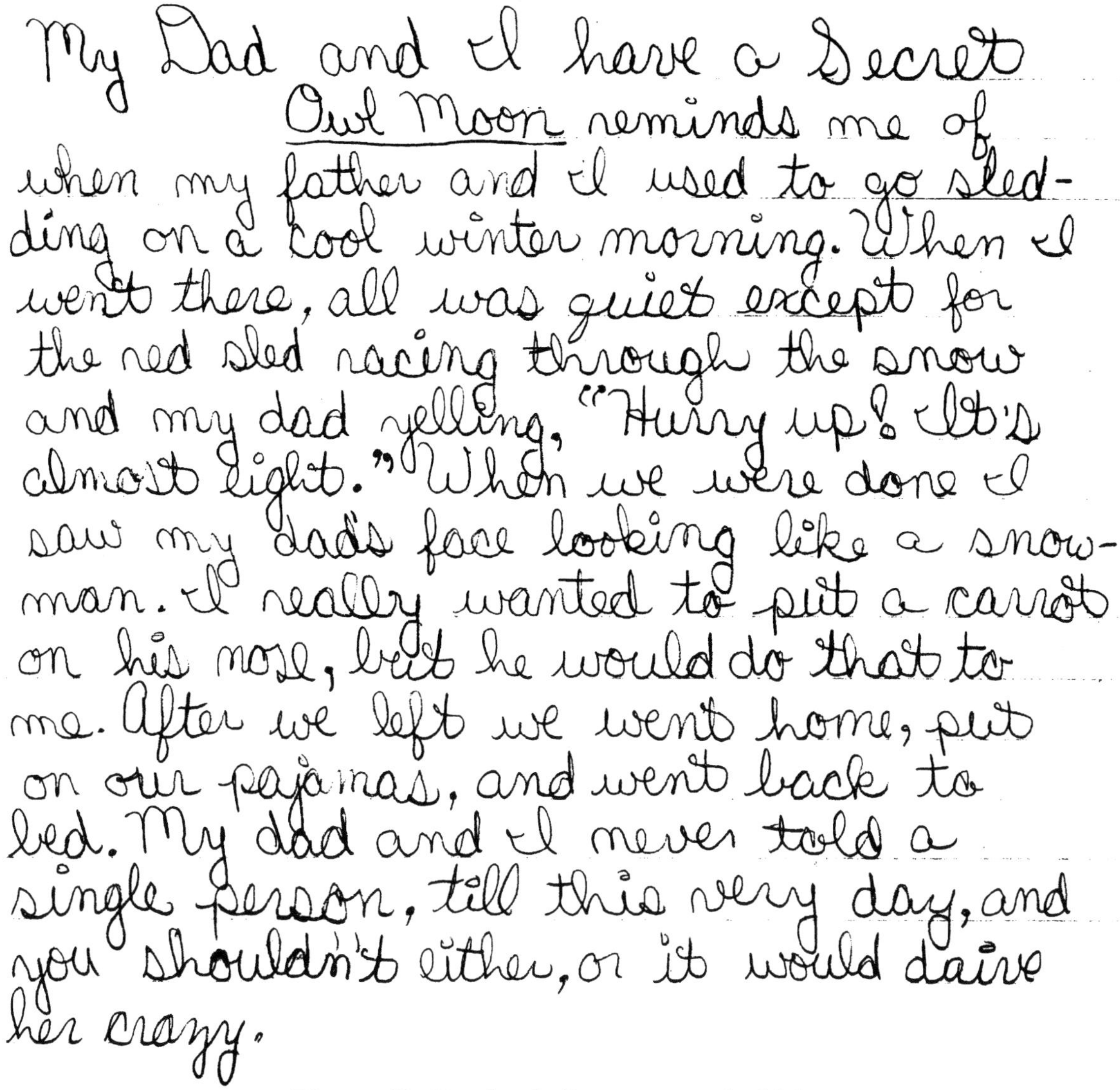

My Dad and I have a Secret

Owl Moon reminds me of when my father and I used to go sledding on a cool winter morning. When I went there, all was quiet except for the red sled racing through the snow and my dad yelling, "Hurry up! It's almost light." When we were done I saw my dad's face looking like a snowman. I really wanted to put a carrot on his nose, but he would do that to me. After we left we went home, put on our pajamas, and went back to bed. My dad and I never told a single person, till this very day, and you shouldn't either, or it would drive her crazy.

Figure 19: Daphne's Response to Owl Moon

move. I felt bad because I was leaving the poor clubhouse by itself. Then I said to myself that I must let it go.

As the kids spoke, others interjected with cries of, "Oh, that's too bad!" "I know how that feels!" or "Something like that happened to me, too!" A rapt listener, I helped to move the conversation along with a few questions: "Who has a similar story to share? Who has a different one?" Thomas answered: "I stay at a place in the summer called Kezar Lake. It's a man-made lake. I wrote about that." Then he read his response (Figure 21).

So many stories, so many experiences.... I felt that for these sixth graders, these responses would hook them into reading more books; they might even begin sharing their stories on the playground or in the classroom. If we "let go" of some of our preconceived notions about reading comprehension, we can help kids get involved in literacy. We can help them join "the literacy club" (Smith, 1988) and become lifelong readers. We can live through many stories as we share our responses together.

Writing Warm-ups: Show-Not-Tell

This section describes a writing technique called "show-not-tell." For second language learners, this is an excellent way to develop vocabulary and build a more sophisticated sense of writing. It

Tar Beach reminds me of when my cousin and I went on top of the train that is parked in the parking lot behind her house. It wasn't in New York, it was in

My cousin always jumped to the next cart and she looked liked she was flying. We also climbed up the roof of a big building that looked like a big castle.

We would sit up on the roof and look down at the tiny houses that looked like doll houses. When we would come down to eat the watermelon we would just look down one more time and when we were done we would come back up and just relax.

Figure 20: Gisella's Response to Tar Beach

The Sky in My Hands: Accelerating Academic English through the Writing Process

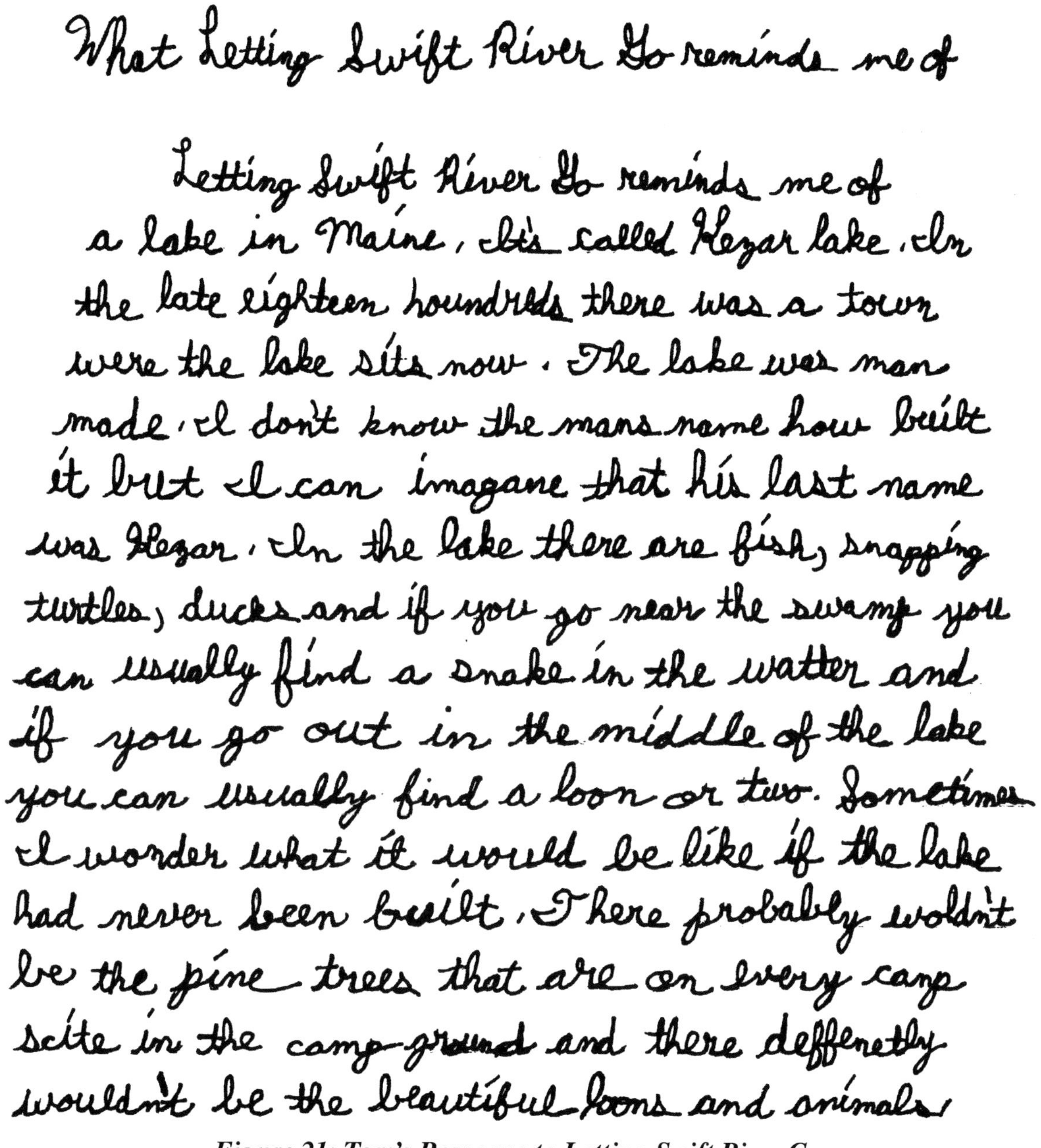

What Letting Swift River Go reminds me of

Letting Swift River Go reminds me of
a lake in Maine, it's called Kezar lake. In
the late eighteen houndreds there was a town
were the lake sits now. The lake was man
made. I don't know the mans name how built
it but I can imagane that his last name
was Kezar. In the lake there are fish, snapping
turtles, ducks and if you go near the swamp you
can usually find a snake in the watter and
if you go out in the middle of the lake
you can usually find a loon or two. Sometimes
I wonder what it would be like if the lake
had never been built. There probably woldn't
be the pine trees that are on every camp
scite in the camp-ground and there deffenetly
wouldn't be the beautiful loons and animals

Figure 21: Tom's Response to Letting Swift River Go

involves describing things with details rather than simply "telling" them.

Angel's piece about Puerto Rico, for example, shows a fairly typical starting point for students I have worked with (Figure 22). Note the vagueness of the details, the elementary word choice (e.g., *stuff*), and the simple sentence construction. Above all, note how the sentences tend to *tell* rather than *show* the reader what Puerto Rico looks like: we do not get any sense of the specifics of the place.

Often, I collect simple writing samples from my students at the beginning of the year. These samples give me an idea of what the students can do and help me determine what kind of writing mini-lessons I need to develop in order to meet their needs. The *show-not-tell* strategy developed by the Bay Area Writing Project, and described in the book, *Wild Words! How to Train Them to Tell Stories* (Asher, 1989), is one that I have found particularly useful. The book suggests that we help kids develop the habit of "showing" things with words by having them "warm-up" each day by

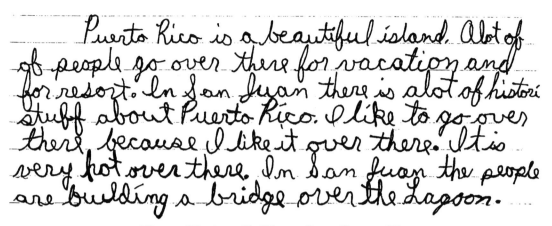

Puerto Rico is a beautiful island. Alot of of people go over there for vacation and for resort. In San Juan there is alot of histori stuff about Puerto Rico. I like to go over there, because I like it over there. It is very hot over there. In San Juan the people are building a bridge over the Lagoon.

Figure 22: Angel's Piece about Puerto Rico

writing showing sentences on the board, sentences that make use of the five senses, action, or dialogue. Introducing warm-ups to students, I typically say, "This is very much like basketball players practicing three pointers; just like athletes, writers need to practice their writing skills, limber their brains to increase their powers of expression."

To demonstrate how authors use the five senses in their writing, I continue this discussion by reading Gary Paulsen's prologue, "Tuning," from *The Winter Room* (1989) or passages from *Your Own Best Secret Place* by Byrd Baylor (1991). We discuss what details these authors use to make their writing come alive. In *The Winter Room*, we can smell the manure on the farm, the hay in the loft, the animals in the barn; Baylor's book brings us to the southwestern desert, where we can see the red of the rocks, the vast, open sky, the coyote hiding behind the rock.

"Do you see how these authors used specific details in their writing to bring us to these special places? The authors showed us these places mainly by appealing to the five senses. Who knows the five senses?"

Roseanne exclaims, "That's too easy! They're seeing, hearing, smelling, tasting, and touching."

"Yes, you're right on the money! Now look at this sentence: *The storm is frightening.* This a telling sentence. It gives us no image of what kind of storm is being described. Adjectives like 'frightening' don't show us the specifics of a storm. In fact, good writing is more about using strong nouns and verbs than about adjectives at all! What kinds of storms do you know?"

"I see a rainstorm! My storm has lots of thunder and lightening in it," replied Earl.

Mark countered, "I like blizzards best: then there's no school!" Everyone cheered at this prospect.

"Now imagine a storm that you have experienced and remember it with all your five senses. Write for five or ten minutes in your journal, showing us your storm with vivid details. Don't leave anything out! Maybe your storm happened here or maybe it happened in Puerto Rico. Bring us there. See what you can do."

As the teacher and I walked up and down the aisles, we helped students who were stuck or were still writing, encouraging them to tell us about the storm they envisioned. Often, voicing their ideas aloud helps students to clarify their thinking. In a conference with Dan, he read this opening: "As I walked home I felt the wind blow. The cold rain hit me. It was like a punch, and the leaves and small branches blew into my face."

"Wow, that's a great beginning. Could you describe your neighborhood for me, since I've never been to your home. What did you see along the way? Were you alone? Try to add more specifics;

Telling
The storm was frieghtening.
showing by 5 senses
I see
I hear
I smell
I touch
I taste

I see lighting, and houses burning, trees falling people running for there lifes. I also see things flying into the tornado people holding onto anything they can. I hear the police cars and people running and screaming. I could see and hear the people running everyone is scared. I smell smoke and I get very nervous. I see the smoke coming from my room I look out the window and saw lighting rood. I ran out of the house. A lighting rood a hit my room the house was on fire I could felt the warm air coming from the buning house. After the storm I tasted pizza with warm coco. I touch what is left from my house it is still warm just like my cup of hot coco. I still smell smoke.

Figure 23: Roseanne "Shows" a Storm

THE OCEAN STORM AND WHAT I SEE

The Ocean was quite and still I
see the clouds come in and get
darker and darker. I get very scared
I Run and try to get help because I
get stuck inbetween to rocks. I
see the waves getting bigger and
bigger. The ocean waves get darker
it stars to rain I scream a bolt
of lighting stricks a house near
me I see it burning I try to
get out of the rock. I get out I'm
safe I run I see everything
going nuts the Ocean starteds
going round and round but
it was going backward everything
came up from the Ocean I
saw lots of ships coming up
They looked like pirate ships
the storm started to go slow
and slower it stop. The ships
got washup in the ocean bay
I run and I went to the
ship I found a treasure I said
to my self If I keep the treasure
I could help my family because
there house had burn down so I
did. The ships were rebuild and
put in a museim.
THE END

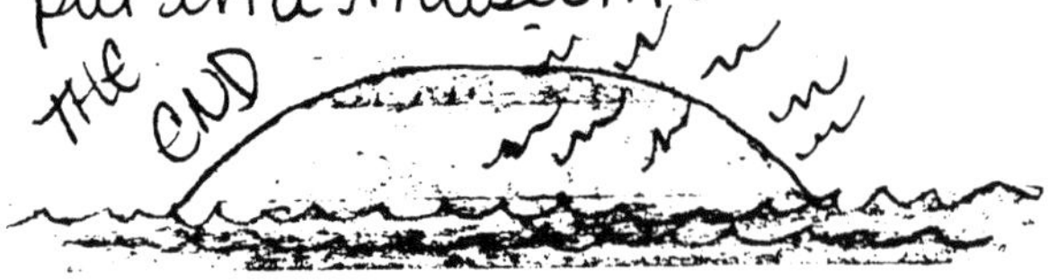

Figure 24: Roseanne's Imaginary Storm

you're off to a great start." I try to limit these kinds of content conferences to two minutes or less so I can give feedback to the thirty other kids. Nonetheless, I find that through conferencing I can give second language learners the extra push of encouragement or clarification they need.

Near the end of the period, we shared our responses. Roseanne, of course, wanted to share hers first (Figure 23). The whole class enjoyed hearing her sounds of police cars and people running and screaming. As we heard about other storms, we were transported into Angela's city blizzard with snow covering the hydrants, Elana's thunder and lightening storm, and Mark's Hurricane Bob experience in New Hampshire. We learned from each other's perspective and relished the images that each brought to life.

The classroom teacher followed up these exercises every day, and the improvements that resulted were palpable. Roseanne wrote a follow-up storm story that took place completely in her imagination (Figure 24). Notice the improved detail here. I especially like her vision of pirate ships and ships ending up in a museum. She is beginning to incorporate the five senses into her stories.

Special Places

We all have special places that we remember in our hearts. These places are sometimes associated with family outings or vacations, but sometimes they are quiet places where we like to go to think or daydream.

Sometimes I read poems to create a mood in the classroom, to evoke daydreams of special places. Previously, I had used Nikki Giovanni's poem (1973), "knoxville, tennessee," to demonstrate to students the use of the five senses in poetry. Now, I used the same familiar poem to evoke a sense of place, a season—in this case, summer at her family's house, which brings us warm thoughts of the south.

"Did you notice the specific details that Giovanni uses to evoke the five senses? She doesn't just mention food; she gives us visions of okra, cabbage, and barbecue; she gives us the feel of going barefoot and the sounds of gospel music. We are taken to Tennessee with all our senses. Can you bring us to your special place? Maybe it's a vacation place that you return to every year, maybe it's a tree house in your backyard, or maybe it's your garage or attic. Try a poem today using the five senses. Perhaps you want to use a pattern of a repeating line, or you may want to create more of a mood in your poem."

Angel asked if he could write about Puerto Rico again.

"Of course, you may. Often writers look back in their journals and find poems or stories they want to revise. What a great idea!"

Notice the vast improvement in the details that Angel included in his poem (Figure 25), compared to his earlier rendition (Figure 22). He is beginning to practice the craft of writing.

Emily chose to write about Guatemala again. This theme turned up in much of her writing, but each time she wrote she introduced us to a different aspect of her special place:

Past the mountain, where you see birds
Climb up and there is my special place, where it is quiet and you can see and hear the
*   birds, crickets, and frogs.*
My place is where you can smell the fresh air, where you can taste the apples and relax.
*   Up there is my tree house in Guatemala.*
I remember when I made that house in the small oak tree.
In my tree house you can touch the rough, rigid walls. You can see the fish jumping out
*   of the water. I climb down when I hear my aunt calling me so we can see the sun*
*   go down.*
After we see the sun go down, I go to my other special place, my room, so I can take a
*   nap.*

These poems helped us to recreate our memories, piece by piece. I am reminded about my con-

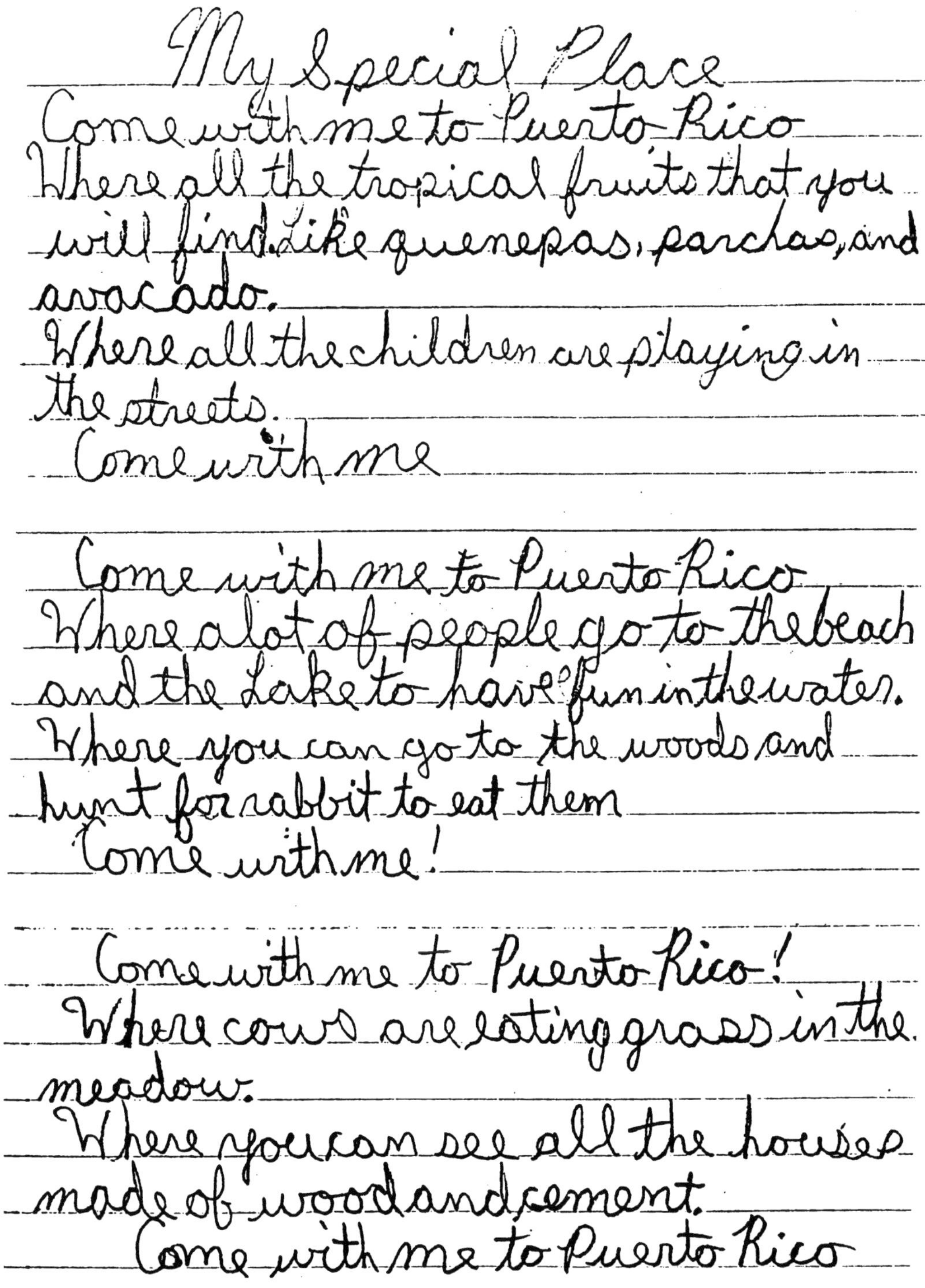

My Special Place

Come with me to Puerto Rico
Where all the tropical fruits that you
will find. Like quenepas, parchas, and
avacado.
Where all the children are playing in
the streets.
　Come with me

Come with me to Puerto Rico
Where a lot of people go to the beach
and the Lake to have fun in the water.
Where you can go to the woods and
hunt for rabbit to eat them
Come with me!

Come with me to Puerto Rico!
Where cows are eating grass in the
meadow.
Where you can see all the houses
made of wood and cement.
Come with me to Puerto Rico

Figure 25: Angel's Poem on Puerto Rico

versation with Walter Dean Myers, who said that as he worked on his novels he surrounded his workspace with objects to reflect his characters; this helped him to shape his story. As I relayed this story to my students, I encouraged them to bring in objects or photos that would help them pull out the details from their memories; these details would improve their writing and help them with later revisions.

Setting

As we explored places and wrote more with the five senses, it was only a short jump to an exploration of setting. We read excerpts from such books as *The Secret Garden* (Burnett, 1998), *James and the Giant Peach* (Dahl, 2000), and *Secret City U.S.A.* (Holman, 1993) to show how authors create believable settings through their attention to detail.

"Do you see that as we read now, we are beginning to read like writers? We are looking at the author's craft to see what we can learn about writing and how we can write better. I'm going to read to you now from the beginning of Chapter Three of the book *The War with Grandpa* by Robert Kimmel Smith (l984). This passage contains an excellent description of a child's bedroom. As I read, think about your room and listen to the details in this piece."

"What are some of the details that you remember about this room?"

Tom called out in his usual exuberant manner: "I remember the high-intensity lamp, the shoe-boxes with the baseball cards, the Hank Aaron poster and the rug that tickles his feet. My room isn't like that at all. It's messy and crowded!"

"Yeah," Andre replied, "His room is smelly, too!"

As the laughter subsided, I said, "Let's try an experiment today. First, describe in your journal the way your room looks, describing it using the five senses. Then, for homework tonight, sit in your room for ten minutes, observing your room with all its littlest details. If it's around suppertime you might begin smelling supper or hear pots clanging. Then, tomorrow, we'll compare the two pieces of writing and see which has more detail."

When I entered the classroom the next day, there was tremendous excitement. Kids were reading their pieces to each other, exclaiming over the descriptions of each other's rooms. I asked, "What did you discover as you wrote in your room last night?"

Tom answered, "My piece is much better now. I included a lot more details. It's a lot easier to write about something when I'm right there" (Figure 26).

Others gave similar replies. They all noticed an improvement in the detail of their writing, and they were proud of the work they had done.

This kind of practice reinforces the notion that writers are observers. I agree with Donald Murray when he says, "Most writers are exceptionally aware of the world around them. Writers have many ways of extending their awareness and connecting what they learn with the past, the present, and the future" (l985, p. 11). I encourage students to be observers of the world around them by observing places, people, and things. I share some of my own observational habits with students—for example the way I can never eat in a restaurant without imagining the stories behind the families sitting around me; I especially observe mannerisms and body language. I want students to know that I am constantly aware of my surroundings and I never know when these details will pop up in a poem or a story; this is the element of surprise that makes the writing life so exciting!

Showing by Action

As Bobby rode on his skateboard down the street he started to do lots of tricks he knew. He jumped over a tire and landed without even losing his balance. Then he went up a ramp and spun around while in the air. Next, he turned around, went a distance away, and started back at the ramp, went up it and jumped into the air as high as he could. Then he skateboarded away.

Now we can see how Bobby was a show-off!

Alyssa wrote the above in response to a prompt that asked her to show the action behind the telling sentence, "He is a show-off!" On the day she wrote it, I walked in to the classroom combing my hair, twirling around, and preening myself. Amid lots of laughter, I asked, " How am I acting? What can you tell about me?"

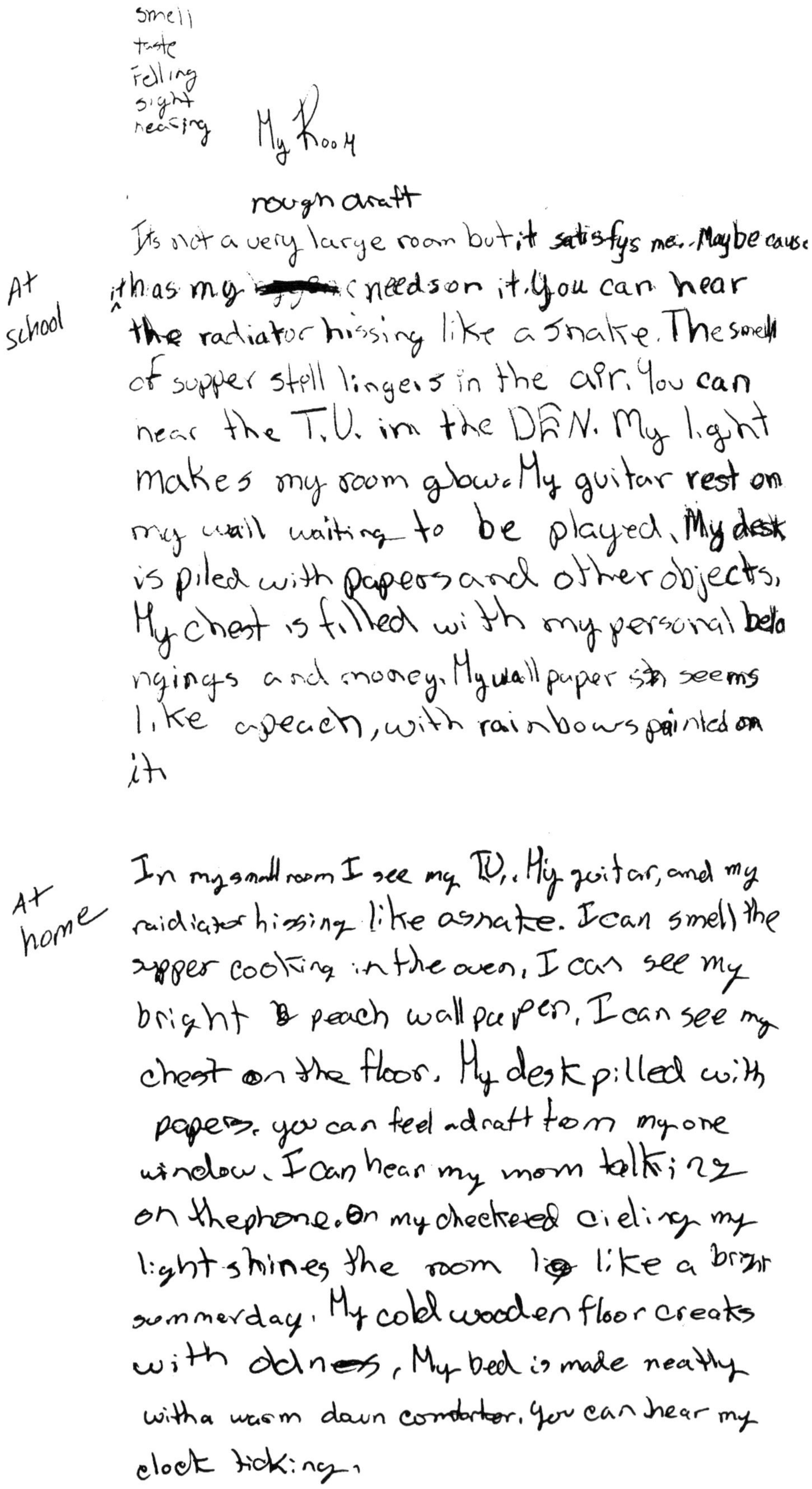

74

smell
taste
Felling
sight
hearing

My Room

rough draft

Its not a very large room but it satisfys me. Maybe cause it has my ~~stereo~~ cneedson it. You can hear the radiator hissing like a snake. The smell of supper still lingers in the air. You can hear the T.U. im the DEN. My light makes my room glow. My guitar rest on my wall waiting to be played. My desk is piled with papers and other objects. My chest is filled with my personal belongings and money. My wall paper still seems like a peach, with rainbows painted on it

At school

At home

In my small room I see my TV, My guitar, and my raidiator hissing like a snake. I can smell the supper cooking in the oven. I can see my bright & peach wall paper. I can see my chest on the floor. My desk pilled with papers. you can feel a draft from my one window. I can hear my mom talking on the phone. On my checkered cieling my light shines the room like a bright summerday. My cold wooden floor creaks with oldness. My bed is made neatly with a warm down comforter. You can hear my clock ticking.

Figure 26: Descriptions of a Room from Memory and in Person

Mike shouted out, "You are acting stuck-up, like a snob. You think a lot of yourself."

"Yeah," said Elana, "I see people like that every day. They think they're so fresh!"

Asking for volunteers to walk their best show-off walk, we howled with laughter as each imitation became more and more vivid. Many boys wanted to imitate girls and vice versa. We brainstormed a list of possible dynamic verbs to depict walking, like stroll, saunter, swagger, and swivel one's hips. Adolescents are acute observers. Such role-playing exercises, together with encouragement to focus on dynamic verbs and nouns, help to transform their observations into vivid writing. Later, Gilberto wrote the following in response to the same prompt:

Brian went to the park and started to dribble the basketball in front of three girls. He started flexing his muscles, then did a flip. He went home and started playing Nintendo and teased his brother and body slammed him. He started talking about himself. Then Brian started drawing some pictures. When he got to school he did thirty push-ups.

Now, that's a show-off! As students like Gilberto and Alyssa began to write more clearly, they practiced the craft of writing while enjoying the power of their words and their impact on their audience. Thus, they showed by their actions that they were beginning to think like writers.

Characterization

Authors reveal characters to us in many ways, but one of the most commonly used ways is by revealing their actions, or by revealing the actions of minor characters towards the main character. *Felita* by Nicholasa Mohr (1979) is one of my favorite books to read aloud. After reading a passage that shows neighborhood kids tormenting Felita by calling her "Spic" and telling her to go back to her own country, I ask, "What kind of kids are these? Have you ever met anyone like this?"

Lots of hands waved and kids responded, "They're mean and prejudiced. They only judge people by their color."

Adam responded by telling a story, "When I first moved here, I went to my next door neighbor's house to introduce myself. When the lady opened the door, she took one look at my black face, and slammed the door in my face, saying we don't want any. It made me feel bad. I know how Felita must feel."

"Yes, I know what she's feeling, too, Adam, because I used to be called "Greaseball" because I'm Greek. I also know how she feels because the author shows us by writing strong dialogue using strong verbs. We can easily identify with the characters."

After that day, the kids begged me to read *Felita*. When I read the passage in which Abuelita gives Felita advice about bullies and prejudice, the class actually stood up and cheered. When students respond to books this strongly, I know they have become hooked on reading. At this point, they begin to realize that the author's words can move us to strong emotions. When I asked students to respond to the question, "What kind of person is the grandmother?" there was no hesitation. Answers poured out, "Kind...loving...wise...strong...smart...brave...caring...proud!"

Reading and writing stories that connect with our lives empowers students to become stronger, prouder, wiser, and more caring about each other and themselves. Literacy is the most powerful tool of liberation that we have to share.

Becoming: A Beginning Look at Our Identities

I am a paintbrush full of vibrance.
I am a clock ticking every second.
I am a smile on a dark, gloomy day.
I am a tulip sensitive but always standing tall.
I am the wind roaming the world, exploring.
I am a bridge holding up all who pass by.

I am a raindrop that falls upon the soft grass.
I am a sponge absorbing different feelings.
I am only human.

Julia's use of metaphor here is startling. A gifted artist, a kind and gentle person, Julia's choice of words in her poem reflects these qualities perfectly. As she develops her other poems and her longer self-portrait, I can clearly see her artistry with words. Julia is as colorful with words as she is with paints.

Young adolescents like Julia love to talk about themselves. Every act of writing reveals more and more about themselves; some artists even assert that in the act of creation we reveal yet another aspect of ourselves. As they write their "Who Am I?" poems, I ask students to choose images that reflect the unique person that they are.

"If you are a person who has a hard time controlling his/her temper, what in nature could you compare yourself to?"

Elizabeth volunteered, "A volcano—you know how it explodes and blows its top."

"That's a great image, Elizabeth. Who has another idea?"

Karina answered, "How about an earthquake? It explodes, too. It destroys everything with its temper!"

As students listened to each other's answers, one idea bounced off another. This initial discussion period is vital in developing students' repertoire of ideas. They begin to see the possibilities for their own writing. Listing their ideas on the board, I asked,

"Now, let's look at the opposite kind of person, a person who is calm, quiet, and reflective. What images could we find that would represent such a person?"

Luis suggested, "A stream in the woods. That sounds quiet to me."

"Great idea, Luis! What other places are quiet or peaceful?"

"Sitting under a palm tree on the beach is peaceful to me. It's so relaxing!" answered Linda.

"In your 'Who Am I' poem today, think which images match your personality. Remember that you are choosing metaphors to represent yourself."

As students wrote in their journals, I noticed how easily they came up with images for themselves. They seemed to know intuitively what represented them best. Flor was having a problem, though. He couldn't think of anything to write.

"Flor, what kind of person do you think you are? Are you quiet and serious, or are you more active and outgoing?"

"I'm not quiet, you know that! I'm always getting into trouble for talking out and getting out of my seat."

"Well, could you say that you are a car that never runs out of gas, or a basketball that bounces down the court? I bet you could think of other images from sports or cars that could represent you?"

"Yeah, I wanna be a Porsche, fast and slick. And Michael Jordan dumping those three pointers. That's me, all right."

Some students, like Flor, need constant encouragement. A few questions often help them get "unstuck" so they can begin writing. On the other hand, students like Julia only need a few minutes of discussion to get them off and running on their own.

My Special Person and Place

In succeeding writing workshops, we further explored our identities by writing poems about special people and places in our lives. I read *Koala Lou* by Mem Fox (1988) and asked the students to think of someone in their lives who made them feel special, just like Lou's mom in the book. I modeled a response by telling them about my grandmother, who "…made me feel unique and loved. She had nicknames for me, she spoiled me rotten, and most importantly she encouraged me to become a

Figure 27: Julia's Special Place Poem about China

teacher. She never gave up on me. Who in your life is like my grandmother? Maybe it's your mom or cousin or grandfather. In your poem today, describe this person for us. Show us how this person makes you feel loved."

Eddie wrote about his grandmother in New York, who had "wrinkles on her face just like the currents of a river"; Rosalba wrote about her father and his delicious *mollejita* with bananas, papayas and paella; Malcolm wrote about his dad and the "pinch of ink in his clothes which he smells when his dad comes home from work." Students had a chance to express love for their families in their poems; I was touched by their sincerity and warmth. In her poem about her mother, Julia wrote about her "hardworking parent striving to support her five children by cleaning, cooking, and caring...her comforting voice urging me on to succeed in school...her sweet, magical perfume...her soft, fluffy white rice…the love between us as we hug each other in happiness." Julia continued to discover bits of herself as she wrote her poems, always impressing me with her attention for detail and her sensitivity as a person.

As a writing teacher, I find this identity project valuable in many ways. First, through poetry students explore a variety of themes from their backgrounds, and each successive poem shows a deepening awareness of detail and a growing facility with language. Second, the exercise allows students to use literature as a springboard for their own writing, which helps them to view reading

My places ....

Past the mountain, where you see birds singing on trees.

Past the lake, where you see fishes, eels, and water snakes.

Past the old tree, that was there when I was born. Climb up and there is my special place, where it is quiet and you can see and hear the birds, crickets, and frogs.

My place is where you can smell the fresh air; where you can taste the apples an relax. Up there is my tree house in Guatemala.

I remember when I made that house in the small oak tree.

In my tree house you can touch the rough, rigid walls. You can see the fish jumping out of the water. I climb down when I hear my aunt calling me so we can see the sun go down.

After we see the sun go down. I go to my other special place my room so I can take a nap.

Figure 28: Emily's Poem about Her Tree House in Guatemala

and writing as flip sides of the same coin. Third, they develop skills that transfer to prose writing when they come to write self-portraits, at which time we work on skills of revision that will be vital throughout their academic careers. Finally, this series of exercises provides students with a well-rounded collection that they can turn into a beautiful self-published book. When I talk to students five years later they still treasure these books.

In writing about special places, Julia chose to write a poem about China. When I asked her if she had ever been to China, she said that she had not, but her mother described China to her all the time and she felt as if she had actually been there (Figure 27).

Emily was inspired by the song "Where I Come From" by Judith Steinbergh and Victor Cockburn (1991). She wrote her own version of the song:

> *Where I come from*
> *We eat beans with rice.*
> *Where I come from*
> *We say, "Buenas noches."*
> *Where I come from*
> *We wear tipico clothes.*
> *Where I come from*
> *Our skin is tan.*
> *Our eyes are light brown.*
> *Our hair is black or brown.*
> *Where I come from*
> *We celebrate Saint Mary's Day.*
> *Where I come from*
> *There are Spanish people.*

In another poem, Emily wrote about her tree house in Guatemala (Figure 28). Each time Emily wrote about her country, she revealed another aspect of her identity. As students explored their identities through poetry and song, they accumulated material for their prose self-portraits. They were encouraged to draw on these poems for the details they would need to write the longer prose piece.

Self-Portraits: The Development of Autobiography

The following week we were ready to begin our longer prose piece. Knowing that many of my students still had problems with paragraphing, I first drew a web on the board with a circle in the middle that said "ME" and asked students for their help (Figure 29).

"If we want to describe ourselves to someone who doesn't know us, what would we want to tell them about ourselves?"

Karyz suggested, "Well, we'd want to describe ourselves first—what we look like."

"Oh, you mean, our physical descriptions," I replied as I connected this topic to the ME on the web.

"What else would we want to know? What do you think, Elizabeth?"

"I think people might like to know if we're funny or quiet, stuff like that."

"Definitely. You mean personality traits. Here, let me connect this to the other side of the circle. Luis, what else do we want to know?"

"How about hobbies or sports? I'd like to write about baseball and the kids I play with."

"Great idea, Luis. Let's connect hobbies to another part of the circle. Now we have three separate topics. Can anyone think of anything else we'd like people to know about us?"

Margarita answered, "What about our families and our favorite foods, or our favorite colors?"

"Sure. You might even use your poem about your special person and expand it to include more details. Or you might decide to have another paragraph about your hobbies and pick one to tell a lot about."

Chapter 5: Developing Our Voices: Inside Sixth Grade

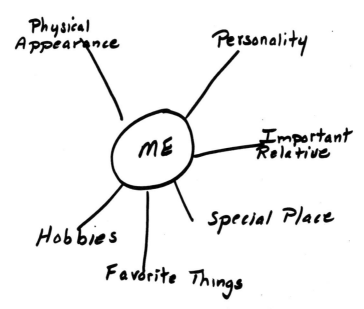

Figure 29: Brainstorming Web for Self-descriptions

We then brainstormed on the board for possible items to be included under each topic. For example, under *personality*, we listed a variety of characteristics: "quiet," "kind," "loud," "sociable," "funny," and so forth; under *physical appearance* we noted many of the possible colors and textures for hair and skin, ways to describe the timbre of the voice, the many shades of blue, brown, and black for eyes, clothing styles, jewelry preferences, etc.; under *places* and *relatives* we listed special people and places from the students' poems; under *hobbies* and *favorite things* we came up with sports, stamp collecting, biking, dancing, colors, and Spanish food. This gave students enough material and inspiration to begin their first drafts; for which I told them that they could begin with any spoke on the web.

As students transformed our web into draft paragraphs, I circulated around the room and asked questions designed to bring out more specific details in their writing. For example, stopping next to Oliver I asked, "What shade of brown? Is your skin tan, cinnamon, or chocolate? Are your eyes a matching color?" And to his neighbor, Elizabeth, I said, "I don't know much about the food you eat if you just say food. Can you be more specific? Is it *arroz con pollo* ('rice with chicken') or *pastelillos* ('meat pies')?" I keep my conferences short and detail oriented so my students can seek out more specific word choices (Calkins, 1994). I learn a great deal about my students from these interactions, and I mean what I say when I leave them with the words, "I can't wait to hear more about you!"

Because our curriculum was just beginning to look at the writing process, most of the kids and even many of their teachers were unfamiliar with revision. In my next mini-lesson, still working with the autobiography exercise, I drew upon my own experiences as a writer:

When I wrote a picture book about my grandmother, my first draft told just the bare bones of my story. I looked over it again to see what details I could add and I started imagining the Haymarket over again as a child, recalling the smells and sounds of the noisy market. Revision helped me 'see my piece again' with a new eye; often I put aside my writing and go back to it after a few days. This gives me distance from my piece so I can look at it more objectively.

A friend read my second draft, and she noticed that my lead didn't hook the reader much, so I worked hard on rearranging my paragraphs and writing a new beginning:

Do you see the changes that I made? Notice all my cross-outs and arrows. Writers don't have time to erase; it interrupts the flow of thoughts. Just a cross-out is fine. Sometimes you might find your new lead in another paragraph in your story, just like I did with my Haymarket story; sometimes you have to start all over again. Did you know that

Michael Crichton rewrote Jurassic Park [1990] seven times until he was satisfied?

Invariably, the kids' initial reaction is "No way! I can't do that. It takes too long." I encourage them by saying that when we make changes in our writing, we are making our writing more beautiful, our stories more interesting: "When you finish, you'll be even more proud of yourselves, and you'll say, 'Look at my story. I did it all, and it looks great!'"

DRAFT 1

The Haymarket

Page 1   Can you imagine a marketplace crowded with push-carts and

wooden crates*^*

~~Can you even imagine these push-carts~~ *piled high* ~~heaped~~ with vegetables,

fruits, and flowers? *Can You are colored lights hang strung before and bud drops on n*

P 2   Can you hear the many languages filling the air, ringing

people's ears with Greek, Italian, Polish, and Yiddish?

→ *Can you smell*

Page 3   When I was a little girl, I visited this marketplace in the

city of Boston, called The Haymarket, every Friday night.

I went shopping there with my grandmother.

Page 4   I called my grandmother, "Yaya", which is the Greek word for

grandmother. She called me "Sugar", because she said I was so

sweet that I could magically touch her coffee and it would

become sweet! *She wore her hair piled high in a braid on the top of her head. She braided my hair in 2 long braids that hung down my back.*

Page 5   Yaya and I would walk up and down the crowded streets.

decorated

We peered in bakery windows ~~piled high~~ with fancy cakes and

pastries ~~filled with ricotta cheese~~. We went into the

butcher shop, where the ceilings were hung with beef and

dangled with hot dogs.

P5 6   Everywhere we went, yaya spoke and joked with all the people

she met. Sometimes, they just talked with their hands. It

seemed to me that everyone was yaya's friend.

Page 7   But, what my grandmother liked best was looking for

bargains. She never bought anything for the price on the

sign. If the lettuce cost 39¢, she would offer 25¢. If the

push-cart man didn't like her offer, she would just move on

to the next person. She always got her price and her lettuce!

Yaya was a great talker!

Figure 30: Sample Revision of the Author's Text for her Grandmother Picture Book

Draft 2
The Haymarket   by Carol Bearse

Page 1   When I was a little girl, every Friday night I visited a fabulous marketplace in the city of Boston, called The Haymarket.   I went shopping there with my grandmother.

Page 2   I called my grandmother "yaya", which is the Greek word for grandmother.   She called me "Sugar", because she said I was so sweet that I could touch her coffee and it would magically become sweet!

Page 3   Yaya and I would walk up and down the crowded streets. We peered into bakery windows, decorated with fancy cakes and pastries. We went into the butcher shop, where the ceilings were hung with beef and dangled with hot dogs.

Page 4 Outside, we saw push-carts and wooden crates piled high with vegetables, fruits, and flowers.

Page 5 Sometimes, in August, the streets were decorated with colored lights. Yaya said that the lights were hung to celebrate the feast days of Saint Anthony and Saint Rocco.

Page 6 I thought that yaya was very wise and knew about lots of things. I wanted to grow up to be just like my grandmother   .

Page 7 It seemed to me that everyone was yaya's friend. Everywhere we went, yaya spoke and joked with all the people she met.

Figure 31: Second Revision of the Author's Grandmother Text

In writing their self-portraits, students almost always begin their first drafts with "Hi, my name is…." To help them reorder their paragraphs, I suggested that they find new ways to begin: "What's your favorite paragraph? Maybe you could begin there!" Emily asked, "What about starting with my special place paragraph about Guatemala? "

"That would be great, Emily. You know so much about this topic that your lead could really hook the reader. Try it and see how it sounds."

Oliver, who was having trouble, needed a few more suggestions: "Oliver, I know how much you love baseball. What if you started with an action lead, showing us the excitement and movement of baseball? Do you think that would work?"

"Yeah, I could tell about the time I helped to win an important game. I already wrote a little about it. I could add more."

"Good for you, Oliver! You see, you had your lead buried near the end. Now, move it forward and

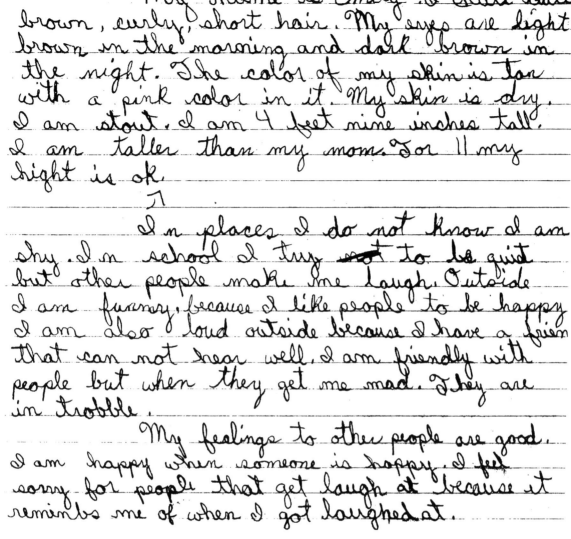

DRAFT 3

My name is Emily. I have dull brown, curly, short hair. My eyes are light brown in the morning and dark brown in the night. The color of my skin is tan with a pink color in it. My skin is dry. I am stout. I am 4 feet nine inches tall. I am taller than my mom. For 11 my hight is ok.

In places I do not know I am shy. In school I try not to be quiet but other people make me laugh. Outside I am funny, because I like people to be happy. I am also loud outside because I have a frien that can not hear well. I am friendly with people but when they get me mad. They are in trobble.

My feelings to other people are good. I am happy when someone is happy. I feel sorry for people that get laugh at because it reminbs me of when I got laughed at.

Figure 32: Draft Three of Emily's Prose Self-portrait

renumber your paragraphs. You're off to a great start!"

Knowing my students as writers and as individuals helps me give suggestions quickly. Since I'd worked with these students all year, I knew quite a bit about them through their writing. Their writing helped inform my teaching.

To help the students write more effective openings, we spent several mini-lessons on how authors write leads. On an overhead, I wrote the four basic lead types that authors use: Description, Background, Conversation, and Action. Borrowing a piece from Meredith Willis' book *Personal Fiction Writing* (2000), I showed them how this author wrote four different leads for a piece that she was writing. I asked students to match these leads to the four general types mentioned, and as I did so, I emphasized that authors experiment with their leads because they want to "hook" the reader into their writing.

Another way to demonstrate effective leads is by reading from some of my favorite books. For a *background* lead, I often read the beautiful beginning of *Missing May* by Cynthia Rylant (1992) or the wonderful lead used by Gary Soto for his story "Two Dreamers" in *Baseball in April* (2000). A lead is much more than one sentence. Often, it is the entire first paragraph. Pointing out that background leads usually tell something about family history or places, I suggested that some students may even want to begin their self-portraits with their special relative paragraph or their paragraph about a special place.

Extending this discussion, we looked in books for other leads, and students began to see how authors craft their stories. Over the years, I have also jotted down on index cards effective leads that I have encountered to use as models for students. As a resource, these cards are a huge time-saver. Moreover, pointing out to students that, as a writer, I am always looking for leads helps them to see that writing and reading are on going, interrelated processes. Experimenting with different beginnings is only part of the fun!

For a *descriptive* lead, I often read from the picture book, *Amazing Grace* (Hoffman, 1991), which begins with the sentence, "Grace was a girl who loved stories" (p. 1). For its simplicity and its directness, this lead can't be beat. Students can adapt this model by starting their self-portraits with sentences like "Danny is a boy who loves baseball." For a lyrical descriptive lead, I read from Jane

DRAFT 4

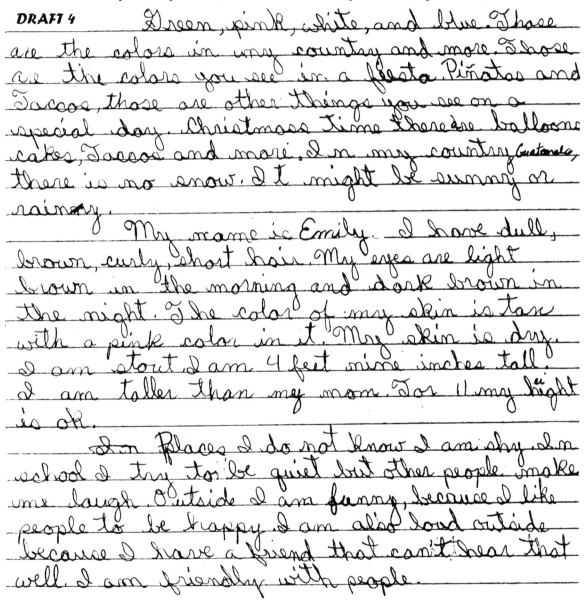

Figure 33: Draft Four of Emily's Prose Self-portrait

Yolen's beautiful book *Letting Swift River Go* (1995), which begins with the sentence "When I was six years old the world seemed a very safe place" (p. 1). This lead combines both background and description. Often there is no "definite" differentiation between these two kinds of leads. The main characteristic elements in both are attention to detail and use of descriptive language.

For an *action* lead, my favorite model is Judith Viorst's book *Alexander and the Terrible, Horrible, No Good, Very Bad Day* (1972). This beginning is terrific for its string of verbs and its emphasis on showing by action. For *dialogue*, *Charlotte's Web* (White, 1974) draws us into the scene with its conversation between Fern and her mother. The book's first page is a masterful example of how to set the tone for an opening chapter.

When I began to read succeeding drafts of the students' self-portraits, I was impressed by the variety of leads. The students had worked hard and were proud of their achievements. We shared our beginnings with each other:

Daphne began: "Vermont! Isn't it a wonderful place? It has clean air, no litter on the ground, and not much pollution. I love the cool breeze and beautiful sunsets. Wild flowers grow freely without anyone there to destroy them...."

Emily wrote: "Green, pink, white, and blue. Those are the colors of my country and more. Those are the colors you see in a fiesta. Piñatas and tacos, those are other things you see on a special day." Emily had indeed worked hard on her revisions. Notice the difference between her third and fourth drafts (Figures 32 and 33).

Emily has added details, combined sentences, and revised her lead; she has grown as a writer through the revising process.

Tom began: "'He looks like a Tommy,' my mother said. 'Christine, he looks like Roger!' said my grandmother. 'Wah! Wah!' cried the no named baby as my mother held me in her loving arms.' For voluble Tom, this was a perfect lead; it inspires curiosity and tells the reader that Tom's talkative streak began as soon as he was born!

Oliver wrote: "Bottom of the ninth inning. Oliver up to bat with two out, two strikes, bases loaded. A tie game 20-20. It's a pitch. It's going, going, gone! I had just helped my team win the championship!" Oliver had picked up on my suggestion and had written a great lead that captured the reader's interest right away.

As students proceeded through this exercise, they began to see that revision was not so much work as it was experimentation. I tried to push them toward this view by sharing comments on revision from such invaluable books as Donald Murray's *Shoptalk* (1990) and Pamela Lloyd's *How Writer's Write* (1987). I also keep a file of author interviews that I cut out or copy from professional journals, *Poets & Writers* magazine, Scholastic Book Club notes, and book jacket covers. These anecdotes help students see themselves as writers.

Another mini-lesson might focus on the writing of conclusions. I have found that this is a particularly difficult task for sixth graders; they often just end their pieces, leaving the reader hanging with no summing up or tying the piece together. I view this as a developmental task, one that beginning writers should work on gradually over the years in middle school.

In introducing the topic of conclusions in this context, I write, on an overhead, four possible strategies that writers can use to conclude their works: *repeat the main idea, make a recommendation, end with the last event,* and *use a quotation.* For their self-portrait, students may want to connect their beginning with their ending, even repeating some of the phrases from their lead. They may also want to sum up for the reader the general impression of themselves that they want the reader to take away. Another effective technique might be to connect the last paragraph to the conclusion so that the reader is left with a general impression of what's most important to the writer.

For examples of the writer's craft, I often read out loud conclusions from picture books like *My Great-Aunt Arizona* by Gloria Houston (1992):

> *Did you see how Ms. Houston left us with an overall impression of the impact her aunt had on all her students? The reader is left with a warm feeling towards the aunt and we understand the aunt in a more complete and satisfying way. Experiment now with your endings; you may find your perfect ending somewhere else within your portrait.*

By now these sixth graders are much less reluctant to experiment. They approach this next revision

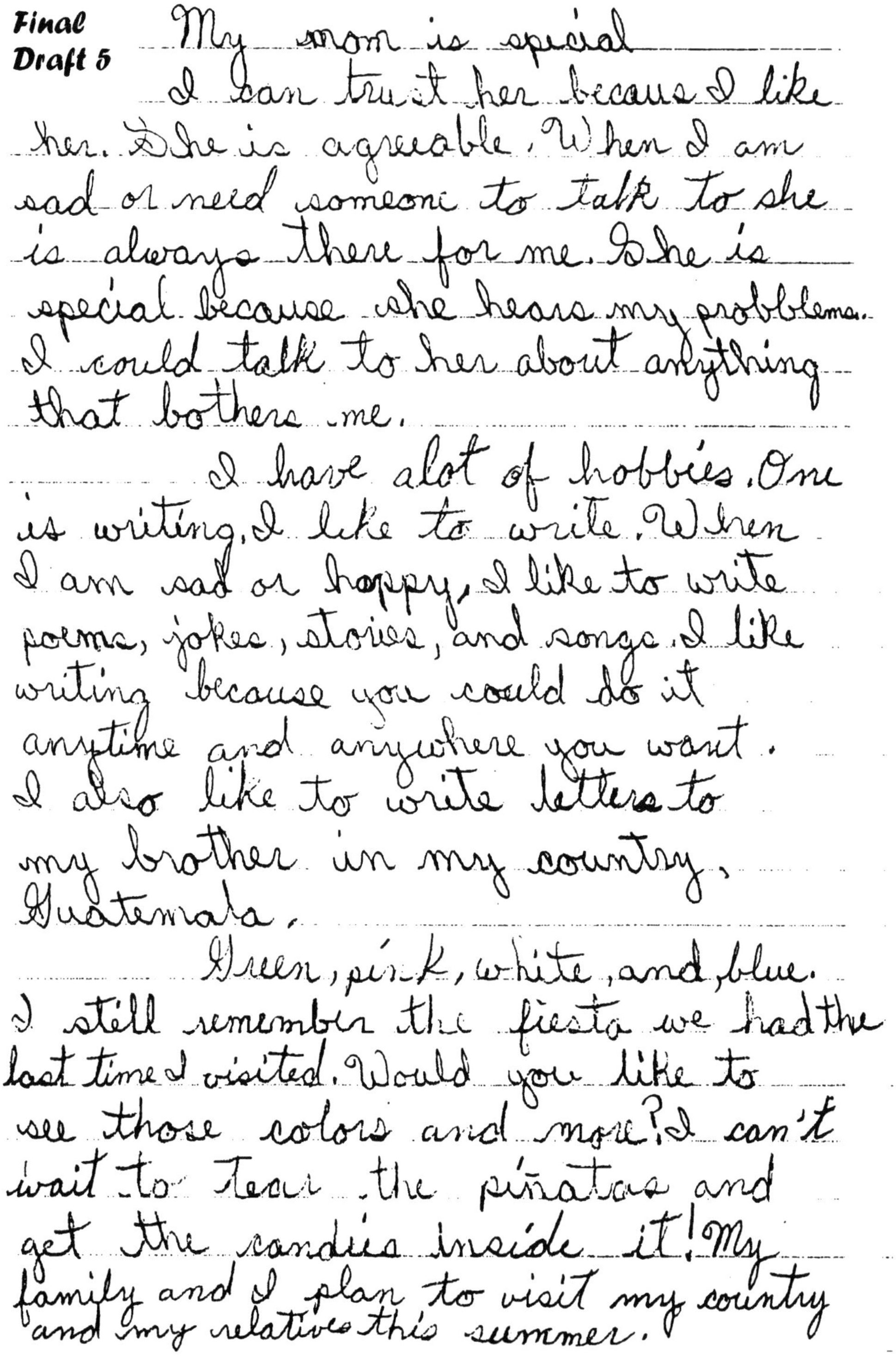

Final Draft 5

My mom is special
I can trust her becaus I like
her. She is agreable. When I am
sad or need someone to talk to she
is always there for me. She is
special because she hears my probblems.
I could talk to her about anything
that bothers me.

I have alot of hobbies. One
is writing. I like to write. When
I am sad or happy, I like to write
poems, jokes, stories, and songs. I like
writing because you could do it
anytime and anywhere you want.
I also like to write letters to
my brother in my country,
Guatemala.

Green, pink, white, and blue.
I still remember the fiesta we had the
last time I visited. Would you like to
see those colors and more? I can't
wait to tear the piñatas and
get the candies inside it! My
family and I plan to visit my country
and my relatives this summer.

Figure 34: Final Draft of Emily's Prose Self-portrait

like "pros," exchanging ideas with their peers as they draft possibilities.

Emily connected her conclusion to her lead, reasserting her love for Guatemala (Figure 34).

Oliver emphasized his love of baseball when he wrote: "I can't wait for spring to come because baseball is back and of course baseball is my favorite sport." Julia summarized the possibilities in her life: "The life I lead is full of excitement and thrills. I lean toward the future ready to face the world and its so many problems, hoping to succeed." As writers, these conclusions were great beginnings for Emily, Oliver, and Julia; they were justly proud of their achievements. In her final reflection, Emily stated: "My self-portrait is the best because I put my feelings into it. I like it because it has a good lead, details, and a good ending. I like it because I have the best paragraph I ever wrote about my mom. That's why I think it's the best."

By the time students typed their self-portraits onto the computer so we could publish them, they were motivated to make their final copy as perfect as possible, and they meticulously checked their spelling and grammar. They were proud and confident. Our school had only five computers, but the Chapter I teacher and I worked out a schedule to ensure that all kids had the opportunity to type their final drafts. Sometimes kids would make appointments and stay after school to finish typing. They all wanted their final pieces to look good. One of the Chapter I teachers confided to me: "I now realize the importance of the writing process. Students are much more motivated to work on their final pieces and when they see how great they look on the computer, they are doubly motivated." For this teacher this was an important realization and I celebrated with her when she discovered the new possibility that writing can bring.

A Possible Rubric

For clarity of expectations, I showed students ahead of time the rubric on the basis of which I would evaluate their writing. I stressed that their pieces would be evaluated in the context of the whole writing process, including the risks they took as they revised. Particularly, I would look at their organization of paragraphs, their attempts at leads and conclusions, and their use of details to make each paragraph come alive. Thus, I tried to tie my evaluation criteria directly to my mini-lessons.

Looking at all the drafts stapled together, with the final draft on top, students could see that their drafting process was important. Because our school still used letter grades on their report cards, I explained that if students had developed all their paragraphs to include details and had taken risks in writing their leads and conclusions, they would get an "A" or a "B." The difference between an "A" or a "B" was usually based on the coherence of the piece; in other words, does it flow from paragraph to paragraph with smooth transitions or does it sound more like five different stories? Wanting my students to be successful—and knowing that they worked harder on this piece than any other piece this year—I was as generous as possible with grades and considering each child's achievement within the context of his or her unique path of development. When I later reviewed my evaluations, I realized that I should have provided more specific comments on each piece of writing. Like my students' writing, these evaluations were beginnings for me, and each time I go through this process I will improve and discover new ways to evaluate student work.

Emily's final draft received an "A" because she took many risks in her writing and developed her paragraphs with many vivid details. Her piece also flows well from paragraph to paragraph. Julia's piece shows a more sophisticated command of the language and reflects her artistic temperament; this was also an "A" paper. Notice, too, Julia's lyrical writing and her strong connection to her roots:

Pow! Firecrackers exploding everywhere I go. As I see the Golden Dragon leading the Chinese New Year Parade, I smile. All the excitement and noise rises in the air throughout the parade. As the noise dies down I can only dream of how wonderful next year's Chinese New Year would be in Chinatown, Boston. The smell of sweet pastries and gourmet dishes fills the air on busy days. Cars are beeping and honking as my family and I try to escape the traffic of Chinatown on Saturdays. Even though Chinatown is crowded and noisy it has been the closest I have come to China, so I love it here.

My name is Julia. My nationality is Chinese. I am proud of my nationality because it is different and unique. I have long vines of black, silky hair that is thick as thread. Looking into my eyes you can discover the depths of a dark, endless cave with no spark of light. The blanket which holds my flesh and blood is faint tan. It is smooth as nylon and soft as clouds. Baggy jeans, dark colored loose shirts are my style. That kind of clothes make me feel comfortable.

With a smile on my face I light up the world being friendly to whomever I see. I am always willing to try and achieve new things. I am sincere to others and deeply involved in my education.

Sketching every detail of life and the world of make believe, I draw my heart out. With my talent each drawing comes to life with a splash of color. My imagination leads me to draw the beauty of art. As I take you into my mind within my drawing you will learn my happy, cheerful personality. Within my hand I hold a talent that will be treasured and with me forever.

Remembering all the times when my mother came to me when I was in pain on the inside or feeling sad I can understand that she cares. She always puts herself last and puts my family and me first. That's what makes her special--she cares. In my life I keep her close to my heart because my mother is special to me.

My favorite thing in life is music. It soothes my mind and relieves my stress. I listen and relax to the comforting beat. As I listen to different kinds of music, I try to understand the meaning behind each song. Understanding helps me deal with life and the problems I face in life. Music is always there for me.

The life I lead is full of excitement and thrill. I lean towards the future ready to face the world and it's so many problems hoping to succeed.

Julia's self-portrait incorporates the many themes that she had already expressed in the poems leading up to this piece. She used these poems as beginning explorations of her identity and as a forum for experimentation with language. With each poem and each draft, Julia revealed another layer of her identity. In Julia's case, her sense of artistry and sensitivity fill her portrait. Her sense of family and pride in her culture are evident, too. I love her uplifting conclusion and how it accentuates her positive spirit!

As the final stage of this project, students created a Cover page, a Dedication page, and an About the Author page for their books. The mini-lesson here emphasized the role of these pages in picture books. Since we are "real" authors, we want our books to look like "real" books. In her book, Julia wrote this moving dedication:

I dedicate this book to my ancestors, the people who come before me. The first Chinese generation to learn the ways of life. The ones who teach my parents to pass on their knowledge to me.

In choosing the best piece of prose for her portfolio, Julia chose her self-portrait. She wrote: "I chose this as my favorite writing piece because I wrote about my life and myself. I think my self-portrait really expresses my feelings and the way I think. In this piece of writing I see the true me, the natural part within the outside."

Adolescents are capable of great beauty and sensitivity. I believe that the middle school years are crucial to the development of writers who are sensitive and observant of the world around them. Their sense of honesty and justice gives them the advantage of being able to write with conviction and moral clarity, and their cognitive and language skills are ripe for polishing and honing. In working with sixth graders, as with all my students, I strive to develop their love of language as well as their ability to craft coherent paragraphs using beautiful prose. I want to help them achieve the lyricism of which I know they are capable.

The next chapter describes oral history and writing for justice projects in seventh grade.

CHAPTER 6

Refining Our Voices, Honoring Our Roots: Seventh Grade Oral History Projects

My primary goals in seventh grade were to build and refine my students' growing repertoire of writing techniques and to help them to expand their writing into longer prose pieces. Oral history projects are one way to connect urban and second language learners to their families and roots and thus to further affirm their identities while achieving these goals. I also wanted to engage my students in interactive reading of novels with stories that would appeal to their sense of justice and their sense of belonging. Foremost in my mind was my conviction that students at this level need constant encouragement and support of their self-esteem, which is challenged and battered by both peer pressure and hormonal changes. Seventh graders are often pulled between their loyalties to family and friends. Writing and reading are two ways to anchor our students to a safe mooring in the midst of a sea of inner and outer changes.

In planning the major writing project for seventh grade, the other teachers and I focused our ideas around the broad theme of choices and family, culminating in the final project of writing an oral history of a family member. This seemed to fit very well with our overall middle school theme of exploring identity and to provide a link between the sixth grade self-portrait and the eighth grade memoir project. In keeping with my conviction that students should read literature connected to their writing projects, I ordered such books as *Dicey's Song* (1982) and *Homecoming* (1981) by Cynthia Voigt, *Scorpions* by Walter Dean Myers (1988), *Roll of Thunder, Hear My Cry* (1984), *The Friendship* (1998), and *Mississippi Bridge* (1990) by Mildred Taylor. These books ranged in reading level from grade 5 to grade 7, thus addressing the need for differentiated instruction within this particular theme of family and social justice. These would be our focus novels for the year. This chapter will describe how I worked with students in responding to the novel *Roll of Thunder, Hear My Cry* and our subsequent work in exploring our families' roots.

To demonstrate to students how oral history is used in writing the history of particular time periods, we planned a trip to the Kennedy Library in Boston. Here students could see firsthand the many artifacts collected and catalogued to tell the life of President John F. Kennedy and his family. Connections like these make writing authentic; students can even think about the possibilities of becoming museum curators or historians. Writing can open many doors for students and they need to see the connections between writing and the real world.

Before we began reading, I brought into class many of the novels of Mildred Taylor and shared with the students many of that author's insights about her writing. I particularly wanted to highlight her impetus for writing: her father's stories.

I felt that for my students, Taylor's words could inspire them to think of their own families in a different way. To help them reflect on their reading of *Roll of Thunder Hear My Cry*, the students kept prejudice journals in response to their reading of the first three chapters, which we often read aloud in order to give second language learners the scaffolding they needed to interact with the text. This writing was done in class over a period of three class sessions. We had many discussions about the historical and cultural context of the Great Depression in the American South, examples of racism as experienced by the Logan family, and the dignity of the characters in the face of adversity. We tied these historical and fictional events to our present times and shared stories of prejudice and adversity experienced living in the city today. In this way students were constantly moving from the book to their own lives and vice versa. Emily wrote the following poem in response to our discussions about prejudice:

> *I'm not black or white, just in between*
> *What does that mean?*
> *It means that I am proud of what I am.*
> *No matter what anyone says.*
> *It means that I stand tall for my country cause I am proud of it.*
> *It means that I am proud how my people live.*
> *It means that I love to walk when I feel bad or good in the big, beautiful, and lively wood.*
> *That is what it means to me!*

In this poem Emily reflected on her experiences growing up Latina; in her writing she continued to articulate her pride in her roots and her love of Guatemala that she began sharing with us in sixth grade. Taylor's book became even more meaningful for her through her *personal* interaction with the text. She identified with the characters' struggles and adopted them as her own.

As we continued to read, students responded in their journals to various prompts. For example, after reading Chapter Four and hearing about Big Ma's special place, I asked them to write about their own special places either in poetry or prose. I often asked them to become one of the characters and write about a particular incident from that character's point of view (*persona*). Emily chose to write in Cassie's voice after reading Chapter Eight. Notice how Emily uses dialect to authentically reflect Cassie's voice (Figure 35).

The powerful ending, "Also they will laugh 'bout a nine year old black girl hitting up a almost thirteen year old white girl," shows how Emily is cheering Cassie on, not only in her battle against Miz Lillian Jean, but against prejudice.

To help them appreciate the beauty of Taylor's language, I had students respond to a passage from Chapter Nine in which Taylor makes us feel spring through the five senses, enveloping us with her words. I asked students to respond by writing about the beauty of spring or another season as they experience it. How would their details be different from Taylor's? How do we experience spring in the city? For inspiration, I read poems like "Just Before Springtime" by Judith Viorst (1984), "In Time of Silver Rain" by Langston Hughes (1995), and "City Rain" by Rachel Field (1926). Jessica responded with this lyrical poem:

> *Spring is coming, here it roar.*
> *Rain and sun and much, much more.*
> *Petals on flowers, leaves on trees,*
> *Nectar for the bumblebees.*
>
> *Spring is coming, hear it roar.*
> *Rain and sun and much, much more.*
> *Grass is growing, birds are hatching.*
> *Come and see spring's warm passion.*
>
> *Spring is coming, hear it roar.*
> *Rain and sun and much, much more.*
> *Clouds are big, skies are blue.*
> *Come and smell the air, spring is new.*
>
> *Spring is coming, hear it roar.*
> *Rain and sun and much, much more.*
> *Hope is growing, love is knocking.*
> *Come and realize that I am talking.*

Can you hear the rhythm of this poem in contrast to Taylor's description of the South? Can you hear the rhythm of the city as compared to the slow, unfolding pace of warmer climates? As writers, we absorb something of our environment, the rhythms that surround us. We are influenced by everything that seeps into our consciousness. As we interact with texts, we translate these experiences into our very own words.

As we continued our reading, I read out loud poems from the Harlem Renaissance, which took

<u>Chapter 8</u>

I can't believe "Miz" Lillian Jean didn't realize it was a game all along. Carrying her books wasn't fun and calling her "Miz" but this was the way to get revenge. She told me some of her secrets 'bout who she liked as a boyfriend and who she couldn't stand. Now if she opens her mouth I'm gonna tell all those secrets of hers.

I told her a lye 'bout something in the forest for her. I didn't thought she would of have hitten me. I went calm and fast and mashed both of us to the ground. (She scratched me on the face but) I kept on hitting her on the right places, like the stomach. I didn't touch her face so nobody know about the fight. I felt good 'bout doing that. I also made her apologize 'bout what had happened in Strawberry's.

If that ole scrawny, chicken legged, snaggle toothed girl tells her Dad, Mr. Simms. Everybody is going to know who she likes as a boy and how she shows it. Also they will laugh 'bout a nine year old black girl hitting up a almost thirteen year old white girl.

Figure 35: Emily's Persona Piece in the Voice of Cassie from Roll of Thunder, Hear My Cry

place around the time in which the novel is set. I read poems by Langston Hughes, Claude McKay, and Georgia Douglas Johnson, to name a few. I wanted the students to see the connection between writing and historical context—to know that writers are influenced by the times in which they live. Thus, poetry is often one of the strongest commentators on history. We wrote poems that were inspired by those we had read, such as this seventh grade collaborative poem based on Georgia Douglas Johnson's poem "Your World" (1989).

> *My world is as big as I dream*
> *I know, for I've dreamed many times*
> *In the deepest reaches of my mind*
> *I dream of a world without crime.*
>
> *Instead, I dream a dream of justice*
> *Where all the people are free*
> *And feel the joy and happiness*
> *to rejoice in equality.*
>
> *I broke the ties that bound me*
> *And I left the past behind*
> *Then I soared up to the mountaintops*
> *Where freedom I will find!*

Taylor's book is filled with the dreams of the Logan family. I urged the students to think about how our hopes and dreams are an important part of establishing life goals. Emily wrote this poem in response to her dreams:

> *Still I Survive*
>
> *As I walk in the rain and thunder*
> *As the rocks that are under scrape my feet*
> *   Still I survive!*
> *As I see violence all around me*
> *As the snake tries to bite me*
> *   Still I survive!*
> *As the bee stings me on my back*
> *As the wind pushes me away from my loved ones*
> *   Still I survive!*
> *As the monster tries to keep me*
> *As the people criticize me*
> *   Still I survive!*
> *As the branch strikes me*
> *As the waves try to swallow me*
> *   I survive!*

Notice how Emily uses symbolism in her poem. When I discussed this poem with Emily she said that the bee, snake, wind, and monster stood for the violence that surrounds her. Another student, Belinda, used the symbolism of color to express her feelings:

> *Color*
>
> *It doesn't matter if you're black or white*
> *It's just the person you are inside.*
> *Color is a stream of brightness and sometimes even darkness.*
> *Color is a piece of beauty that floats around each day that passes.*
> *Color is a string of hair that passes from generation to generation.*

Color is what we live and how we treat it is the way it will treat us.
Color.

Notice Belinda's use of "string" as a metaphor for ancestry and the way she treats color as an animate object. To me, this demonstrates that Belinda has internalized our earlier work in *persona* and applied it in a new context.

Rosenblatt's (1978) transactional theory holds that in order to comprehend a text fully the reader must interact with the text on a personal level. My students' responses to *Roll of Thunder, Hear My Cry* showed them engaging in this process:

Mildred Taylor made this book become real. She is a very good writer. I say she made this book become real because I felt all the pain and suffering inside of me and my body!

Mildred Taylor, the author, made me feel great with a lot of feelings. She's a great author. I never knew a book can make me have so many feelings, sad, happy, mad, and then sad again.

I didn't like how the story ended. It left you with the suspense of what happened to T.J. I felt that she should have written about what happened to T.J. because people really wanted to know. The moral that she tried to teach us is to have a good heart about people and to don't hang around with a bad crowd. To have a good heart so people will like you. Don't hang around with a bad crowd because you could get into more trouble than you already are.

The students also watched the video and compared it to the book. I was pleasantly surprised when their teacher told me that they were unanimous in their vote that the book was far better than the movie! They especially disliked the fact that the movie skips around in its sequence of events and gives an inauthentic version of the school bus incidents. I expanded on their discussions with their teacher by demonstrating the use of a Venn diagram to compare and contrast the video and the book (Figure 36).

The students in this class, the majority of whom were designated as Chapter 1 students, were able to think critically about their reading when guided through a lively discussion. Talking was important for them before they could write. These students also demonstrated to me, once again, the importance of providing time for adolescents to read reflectively and to write in a variety of response frameworks that enable them to relate meaningfully to texts.

When middle school students engage with the characters and theme of a book, they become active readers. They also begin to read like writers, appreciating the quality of the author's writing. I believe that even the most reluctant readers can be drawn into reading through writing. As they strive to become more proficient writers, they naturally want to read other writers to learn from them.

Because of their success with *Roll of Thunder,* students requested further reading about the Logan family and began to read *The Road To Memphis* (1992) and *Mississippi Bridge* (1990). After we had read and responded to Taylor's books, I felt that we were ready to begin our own quest for roots and family. Knowing that some of my students came from fragmented families, I gave them the option of another writing project that involved interviewing adults other than family members. Each student was given a folder for their drafts and collections of photos and other artifacts. The following questions were used as guidelines by students in their interviewing:

1. Ask your family member about his or her childhood. Where was he or she born? How many siblings did he or she have? Where did the family live-- farm or city area? Describe the family home.

2. Describe the schools he or she attended.

3. Tell about one game your family member played as a child and why he or she liked it. Describe his or her favorite outfit of clothes.

4. Does he or she remember any funny stories about school or childhood?

5. How did his or her parents meet? Where?

6. How did his or her family come to America? Why did they leave their native country?

7. How did he or she come to live in this city?

8. How is this place different from where he or she grew up?

9. What hopes and dreams does your family member have for the future?

10. Describe one thing in the home that means a lot to the family and explain why it is important.

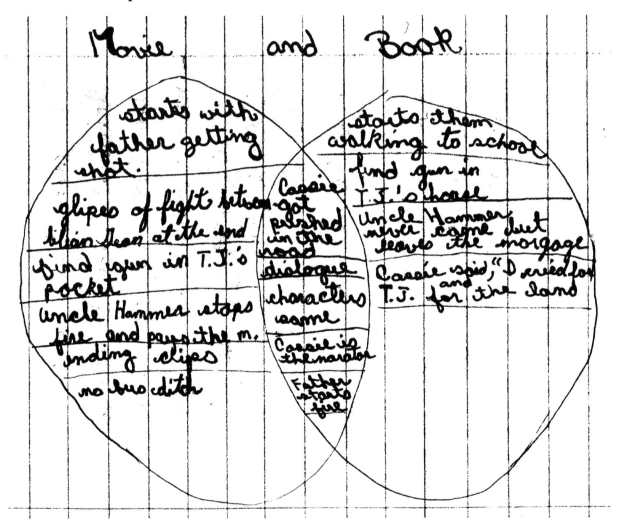

Figure 36: Venn Diagram Comparing the Novel Roll of Thunder, Hear My Cry to the Film Adaptation

I urge the students to take notes as they interview their subjects. If they can tape-record the conversation, that is also very helpful. I also tell them to consider the above questions only as a rough guideline. They are welcome to ask additional questions to obtain further details. These questions might follow such formulas as: *Do you remember…? Describe… for me. How did you feel about…? Tell me about…. Is there anything else?*

As the students were gathering their information, they wrote a variety of poems to help crystallize their thoughts about family. We also drew coats of arms with symbols for things that make our families special and filled in family trees with as much detail as we could. Activities like these help middle school students relate to their families and to the past in ways they often have never considered.

I believe that we take many journeys through our writing. A journey into our past is a sign of growing, of trying to understand why we are the way we are. This inevitably helps us to know where we will go in our future. I helped students on this journey through the writing of poems that became part of their final oral history books. I shared Walter Dean Myers' book *Brown Angels* (1993) with the students to give them an idea of how photographs can inspire poems. I urged the students to bring in old photographs to write about. I brought in many of my own family albums and shared stories handed down to me by my grandmother. I asked the students to bring in family heirlooms as we discussed the gifts that were passed down to us. Often, our most important gifts were not material at all: they were our red hair, our long, silky curls, our athletic and musical talents, or a cherished recipe. After listening to the song "Family Gifts" from the tape *Where We Come From* by Victor Cockburn and Judith Steinbergh (1991), Lisa wrote this poem about her "gifts":

> *The gifts of love and honesty*
> *have been passed down.*
> *We don't let anger*
> *Beat us to the ground.*
>
> *We have pride in our beautiful country*
> *Republicana Dominicana., la tierra de mi corazón*
> *(Dominican Republic, the land of my heart)*
> *All people unite to form one, de los campos hasta la ciudad*
> > *(from the country to the city)*
> *That's how our love helped us win*
> *The gift of love.*

Notice how Lisa deftly weaves in her native tongue to celebrate the Spanish language as one of her gifts. She also reflects the strength of her family values in her poem.

As students brought in their interviews, I helped them draft paragraphs based on their notes. We webbed the various questions on the board and filled in the answers. From the web, students began their first drafts. We spent several weeks drafting, adding details, revising leads, and cultivating varied sentences. Many of my mini-lessons were reviews of techniques we had learned in the previous year; my goal here was to refine what we had learned and especially to work on sentence composing. We looked back at Taylor's books to see how she constructed paragraphs. We noticed how she varied her sentence openings, how she combined clauses into compound and complex sentences, and how she substituted pronouns for nouns. These are the subtleties that empower writers to improve their writing from the basics to a craft.

As I observed Emily drafting her mother's history, I noticed how she wove the colors and sights of Guatemala into her story. Many of these threads were expansions from her sixth grade self-portrait. Emily's family and heritage are important to her; each year she refined and developed these values in her writing. Her final draft (Figure 37) demonstrates her growth in the craft of prose writing.

I believe that it is important to give students opportunities to go back and reflect about what they had written earlier by looking through their writers' notebooks and portfolios. As they explore these themes in another year and through another format, they become able to define their identities and perspectives in stronger, more mature ways. This gives them new confidence and leads them to new levels of technical development.

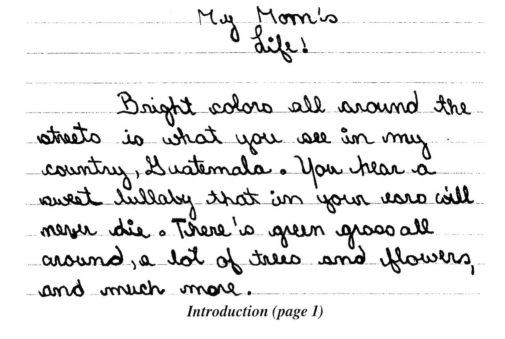

My Mom's
Life!

Bright colors all around the streets is what you see in my country, Guatemala. You hear a sweet lullaby that in your ears will never die. There's green grass all around, a lot of trees and flowers, and much more.

Introduction (page 1)

My mom, Sara, hopes that we become something good in our life. Her dream is to see us grow up healthy and get married. She wants people to like us and respect us. My mom hopes that my brothers and I help each other in the future. She also hopes that we love each other.

Conclusion (page 5)

Figure 37: Excerpts from Emily's Prose Family History

The students in this class loved sharing their oral histories. Indeed, I have found that this exercise has a unique power to develop community in the classroom. Through sharing their histories, students learn to appreciate people from many cultures. They learn also about the universality of family and the power of stories. The following piece by Lisa is one of the many stories that highlighted this culminating process:

My Mother

Beaches, parks, and lakes are places you go in my mother's country. She was born in Republican Dominicana. Her elegant name which her mother heard on a Spanish soap opera is Julietta. Her family consists of eleven siblings: eight girls and three boys. Julietta is the third youngest in her family. Both her parents are Dominican and are alive today.

When my mother was young, she used to live in the countryside in D.R. She loves her country because it's very friendly. Everyone knew each other and was like a big family.

When Julietta was five years old at her sister's wedding, they made her put on a dress from a doll. The dress was white with lace. It was a gorgeous dress. My mom was a little baby when her father brought her in a basket to wherever he had to work on a farm.

When Julietta got a little older, she moved to Queens, New York. She came here in an airplane. At that time you wouldn't come here like you owned the country. You had to get your permanent residence in Canada. Little groups from my mother's family came to America. She was in the last group to come.

My mother lived in Bronx, New York in her own house. My grandmother bought a two-floor house used by the whole family. It's a very nice house. The outside of the house is blue and has maroon bricks. Downstairs there are three bedrooms, a kitchen, bathroom, and living room. Everybody in my mom's family gathered to smell their mother's good cooking. They celebrated each and every holiday.

My mom hopes that this family keeps faith in our Hispanic Culture. My mom wants our traditions to go from generation to generation. Julietta says, 'If you don't know where you came from, you don't know where you are going.'

When I asked Lisa to choose her favorite piece of writing from seventh grade, she chose this piece about her mother. She said, "I chose this story because I got to learn a lot about my mother while doing the interview. We had a good conversation about our country and family. This story brought a lot of memories from when I was young. I love this story because it came from my heart." This is typical of responses from students when asked to choose their favorite piece. The most important consideration for my students was to choose pieces that came from their hearts. In interview upon interview with my students in these three years they told me that poetry appealed to them because their poems came from their hearts, from their deepest held convictions. Oral history, which is indeed a conversation about our family's memories, also delves into the corners of our hearts, as Lisa so aptly expressed it.

I learned many stories from my students that deepened my appreciation for their struggles, hopes, and dreams. I learned from Bounlay about his family's flight from Cambodia to the United States. I learned from Adam that in Africa his name means "string that can't be broken." I learned recipes that had been handed down from generation to generation. I also have renewed hope that old and new immigrants alike share the same wish for their children: that they may hold both respect for their ancestors and dreams for a more prosperous future.

We bound our poems, stories, and photos into books that celebrated our family stories. Many students made collages of photos for their book covers. As students shared their books, I saw them sparkle with animated interest. We were left with a desire to learn more about our past. As I looked forward to our work in eighth grade, I realized that the students could build on their new knowledge to write more detailed memoirs. The next chapter discusses this transition from life stories to memoirs.

CHAPTER 7

Writing Memoir in Grade Eight: The Link to Non-fiction

One summer I became thoroughly captivated by reading and writing memoirs. My adventure began as I read William Zinsser's book *Inventing the Truth: The Art and Craft of Memoir* (l987). I became fascinated with the lives of Annie Dillard, Toni Morrison, and Alfred Kazin. I went on to read their books and traveled with them to Pennsylvania, the deep South, and Brownsville, New York City. On the way, I gained insight into how writers invent themselves through writing. I began to remember my own childhood in the tenements of Roxbury, and a million little details came flashing back: clotheslines strung across neighbors' roofs, cobblestone walks, and walled gardens. Often my memories were exact, but more often than not I reinvented my experiences. As Zinsser states:

> *The writer of a memoir takes us back to a corner of his or her life that was unusually vivid or intense.... By narrowing the lens, the writer achieves a focus that isn't possible in autobiography; memoir is a window into a life. (p. 21)*

It seemed to me that I could help my students achieve this same focus by writing memoirs in eighth grade. It was a logical extension of their oral history work in seventh grade and a further exploration of their identities. I also believed that memoir could validate students' lives and experiences in a profound way while at the same time developing writing that was a close link to non-fiction.

As I worked on developing my own memoir, I realized that I was focusing closely on my grandmother. She became the eyes through which I perceived my childhood. I had written many poems in the past about my grandmother; I had even turned one sestina into a picture book, but until now I had never delved into memoir. It seemed that I had all the beginnings in my earlier poems; now I would bring all the parts together.

A unit on realism that year would become the launching pad for our eighth grade writing. As students were reading Maya Angelou's book *I Know Why The Caged Bird Sings* (l969), we also learned more about Angelou's life by reading her poetry. I wanted to demonstrate to students that by reading both Angelou's poetry and prose we would be able to fully capture the essence of her indomitable spirit.

I brought her books of poetry and autobiography to class. I began by reading her poem "Phenomenal Woman" (1986) in my most dramatic voice, wearing my brightest, reddest dress! Even the most apathetic students were drawn into the rhythm and playfulness of her words. They also sensed her pride, though we had a lively discussion about the difference between pride and conceit! I invited them to write their own versions of this poem, celebrating their unique aspects and even exaggerating their positive qualities. As I conferenced with individual students, many said that they had no "beautiful" qualities; I gently encouraged them, praising them for their curly hair, their smooth mocha skin, their wide smiles, or their sparkling brown eyes. As I circulated, this spirit became contagious and other students shared positive comments about their peers. The following poem by Carlos is one of my favorites to share:

> *Handsome men wonder where my secret lies.*
> *But when I start to tell them,*
> *They think I'm telling lies.*
> *I say,*
> *It's in the fragrance of my skin*

That women like to smell
Whether they're stout or thin
They always ring my bell.
I'm a man
Phenomenally.
Phenomenal man,
That's me.

I walk into a room
Just as cool as you please,
I break through the door
And they fall on their knees.
I say
It is with the romance that I speak,
That girls give a shriek.
That's why my poems are fresh
And your poems weak!

I'm a man
Phenomenally.
Phenomenal man,
That's me.

It's the fire in my eyes
And the flash of my teeth,
The swing in my waist
And the joy in my feet.
I say,
It's in the tone of my voice
And in my thoughts
To be your number one choice
So untie my knots.

I'm a man
Phenomenally.
Phenomenal man.
That's me.

Carlos used Angelou's form and rhythm to create his poem. Once a reluctant writer, now he was finding success by apprenticing with other writers and borrowing their structures to launch his own unique voice. He volunteered to read his poem and the reaction of the class was spontaneous applause along with good-natured ribbing by both the girls and the boys. Carlos's enthusiasm was catching; not to be outdone, of course, the girls read their poems next.

Carlos was not always a willing participant. In an interview at the end of eighth grade, Carlos admitted the following:

> *Last year when you first came [to our class], I thought poetry was for wimps. I gave*
> *you a hard time. There was a lot of peer pressure. After I started writing a few poems,*
> *I noticed I had some talent. I needed someone to tell me that I was a good writer, that I*
> *had talent. One day, Mrs. Bearse told me my poem was great and I had potential. Now I*
> *know writing is not for sissies and I'm not scared to write.*

Carlos is not an unusual case. He is not exaggerating when he says that he gave me a hard time in class. I responded with persistence and patience because I believe that all students have the potential for greatness. With Carlos and many others, this approach paid off.

Carlos is also a passionate and talented artist. In seventh grade he created a wall-sized tropical rain forest mural for our school. In eighth grade, Carlos began to notice the natural connection between art and poetry. In fact, in his interview, he asserted: "Writing and art go together, because you make up your own world. Nobody can tell you whether it's right or wrong—it's what you feel, it's your world."

I often give students a packet of selected poems by Angelou to study and read as we discuss her poetry. I ask students to choose a poem from this packet that they particularly admire. By this time students are more than ready to write on their own, using Angelou's poems as their inspiration. The poem "Still I Rise" (1986) inspired this poem by Jennifer:

> *You may walk all over me*
> *With your high heeled boots,*
> *You may disgrace me with your lies*
> *But still, above it all, I'll rise.*
>
> *Does my happiness upset you?*
> *Why are you filled with hate?*
> *Cause I walk on air like I've got more friends*
> *Lined up at my gate.*
> *Just like the flowers and rainbows*
> *Unbroken by your hate,*
> *Just like peace without any cries,*
> *Still I rise.*
>
> *Did you want to see me crying?*
> *Teardrops falling fast*
> *Crumbled hopes falling down*
> *Shattered dreams blown through town.*
> *Does my giddiness offend you?*
> *Don't take it the wrong way*
> *Cause I laugh like I've got sunshine*
> *On a very cloudy day.*
>
> *You may shoot me with your words,*
> *You may cut me with your eyes,*
> *You may kill me with your hatefulness*
> *But still I rise.*

This poem is a masterpiece of language and rhythm. Jennifer has absorbed the cadences of Angelou's poem to perfection. She has apprenticed well. Marissa, on the other hand, was fascinated with Angelou's inaugural poem, "On The Pulse Of Morning" (1986):

> *I look upon the ocean and see the sun rising above it.*
> *A giant predator overpowering what seems to be an infinite horizon.*
> *Let it be our mother, caressing and comforting.*
> *Let it take us and warm our hearts.*
> *The sun is the mother of us all, no discrimination, nor prejudice.*
> *Let our mother take us to morning.*
> *Stand and look at our mother.*
> *She calls to us.*
> *Here in the pulse of the morning, we listen to her wise words.*
> *"Awake my children.*

Awake upon a new day.
Today my children you shall stand.
Be proud of your heritage whatever it may be.
Just remember that everyday
Your mother will be here to say, with hope,
Good morning.

Marissa, a serious student, makes a strong statement with her poem. In the eighth grade, Marissa's poetic voice developed and deepened. Always a good student, Marissa was often reluctant to take risks in writing poetry. This poem seemed to be a turning point for her; her poems after this were much stronger and were filled with lyrical language. I have found that students seem to intuitively know which poems speak to them; as Rosenblatt (1978) has suggested, students make texts their own when they interact with them in personal ways.

As we read and wrote, Angelou's poetry inspired us to think about people and themes that dominated our own lives. We began exploring our own lives for memoirs by looking for insights from other authors. I shared poems such as those by Tina Pomeroy ("Making Potica"; 1987) and Sandra Cisneros ("Abuelito Who"; 1994) to illustrate the poets' use of the five senses to make people come alive. I used my grandmother poems as points of departure for the class. For my first mini-lesson on writing memoir, I shared my poems on an overhead:

When I remember my grandmother,
I see her silver hair tied in braids on the top of her head. I see her smile that always
*   greeted me with love. I see her black garden shoes that she wore when she dug in*
*   the roses.*
I hear her voice calling me "Sugar." I hear her warning, "Prosexi Kala" which means
*   "Be careful" in Greek. I hear her stories about Greece and about working for two*
*   dollars a week in a factory in Boston. I hear the pride in her voice when she tells*
*   her friends about her granddaughter, the teacher.*
I smell Easter bread baking, chicken soup with lemon, and "koulouria." I smell the food
*   of my ancestors.*
I taste the bitter Turkish coffee and the sweet baklava. I taste my tears as I say my final
*   good-by.*
I touch her rough, work-worn hands, the hands of an immigrant. I touch the sweetness
*   of her smile, the melody of her voice.*
When I remember my grandmother, I touch my past and my beginnings. I touch the
*   Earth.*

I explained to the students that this poem was a working draft for me; many of these details were from other pieces, some became new as I wrote. I discovered new corners of my memory as I wrote. Murray (1990) states:

Awareness makes writing possible…. While we are writing we recognize the significance
of what we remember and what we did not know we remembered, enabling us to 'remem-
ber' what we have not yet experienced. (p. 15)

I suggested to the students that they focus on an adult who has had great importance in their own lives, reminding them that memories often come flooding back in sensual details. Their poem would become the basis for their longer memoir, and we would expand upon our details in successive drafts. Sometimes students expressed their concern over having a meaningful adult to write about; as I conferenced with them, I urged the students to be honest in their writing and pointed out that memoir writing can often be painful, but that through writing about their emotional conflicts, they could come to a greater understanding of both their significant adults and themselves. This

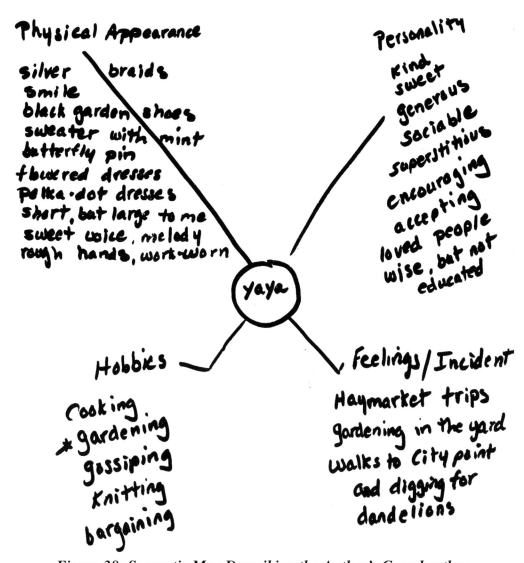

Figure 38: Semantic Map Describing the Author's Grandmother

tension creates the power behind this kind of writing.

I illustrated this in my next lesson. I showed my poem again, and then I presented a semantic map (Figure 38). I shared my process with the students and pointed out that when I worked with a map, I began adding new details that I remembered while writing. Now that I was moving to a longer prose piece, my grandmother needed to be described in greater detail. I began with four categories that would provide material for four descriptive paragraphs.

On a blank map, we brainstormed possibilities under each category for the students' significant adults (Figure 39). For example, under physical description, we listed voice (tone or timbre), favorite clothing, hair color and texture, color and shape of eyes, skin color, jewelry, perfume, etc. In many cases, the students found some of these details already present in their poems. Others they could now add, and as they did so I conferenced with them to provide encouragement and to monitor their progress. This also allowed me time to ask clarifying questions such as, "What kind of voice does your father have—deep and husky or scratchy?" or "What kind of gray hair is it—silver, speckled, whitish?" When I asked Lisa to describe her father's bald spot, she responded, "Oh, it looks just like a U turn on the back of his head!" Now I had a definite picture in my mind of this man's head! These are the kind of details that can be nudged from students, and conferencing at this point helps students clarify their thinking.

We spent about twenty minutes going from poem to map. After this preliminary work, we moved

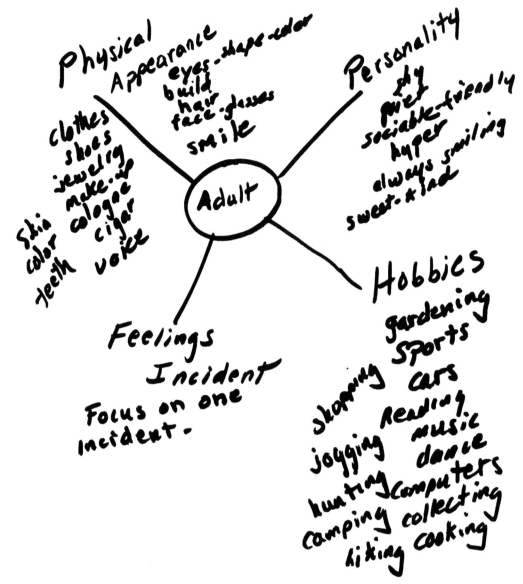

Figure 39: Generic Semantic Map for Personal Descriptions

from the map to writing paragraphs. I have found this to be the most effective method for helping students to organize their thoughts into coherent paragraphs. Even in the eighth grade I encountered many students who either did not write in paragraphs or whose paragraphs were jumbled up with many topics. The semantic map helps them to organize their material since they can see at a glance that each section of the map belongs in a separate paragraph. We started with these basic four paragraphs and then, with each succeeding draft, we added more. For reluctant writers, this basic plan provided a key to their success in writing longer pieces, and for many of my students this memoir would become their longest piece of writing to date. For confident writers, this kind of plan provides only the barest of outlines, but they too have told me that this process allows them to grow, to develop their paragraphs one-by-one and therefore to achieve greater detail and precision.

The next few mini-lessons were spent on clarification, expansion, and addition of details. I often put on the overhead some of the vignettes from Sandra Cisneros' books *The House On Mango Street* (1989) and *Woman Hollering Creek* (1991) because of her incredible use of language and delineation of characters. Jean Little's book *Hey, World, Here I Am!* (l987) is also excellent for demonstrating effective descriptive writing. I pointed out to students how Little shows us Mrs. Buell's sweater in such detail that we can "see" it clearly in our minds. We looked together in the same piece for other places where the author paints word pictures. We also read sketches by Alice Walker ("In Search of Our Mothers' Gardens"; 1987) and Rudolfo Anaya (*Abuelo*; 1983). In addition, as the students were reading Angelou's *I Know Why The Caged Bird Sings* (1969), they worked with their classroom teacher to identify passages where the characters seem to step out of the pages.

I helped the students work on their drafting by focusing the subsequent mini-lessons on specific aspects of the revision process. From their initial drafts, I could see that my students needed specific help in developing their pieces. Despite an immersion in the reading of memoirs, they needed guidance to hone their own pieces. I designed my mini-lessons to focus on the following elements of the writer's craft: 1) rearranging paragraphs for more effective organization; 2) adding details that paint word pictures by showing not telling; 3) crafting effective lead sentences; 4) varying sentence structure; 5) transitions; and 6) conclusions. I also let students know that I would be assessing their drafting process based on how they incorporated such revisions into their final piece, according to the following rubric (Figure 40):

REVISION: What revision attempts were made on this piece by the author?

1. Rearrangement   _____

2. Add details   _____

3. Lead Sentence   _____

4. Varied Sentences   _____

5. Transitions   _____

6. Conclusion   _____

Figure 40: Rubric for Assessing Drafting Process

This showed students that I was interested in the entire process, not just the final product. I found that students were grateful for this kind of guided format; they moved from draft to draft with more ease and sense of purpose; they could see the importance of revision as they saw their pieces grow and improve. I emphasized to the students that revising is like putting a puzzle together: with each piece, the meaning becomes clearer and more beautiful.

For ease of management, the students kept separate memoir folders, which contained their poems, semantic maps, drafts, and conference notes. I have also found it helpful for students to write paragraphs on separate pieces of paper, skipping lines for ease of revision and comments. Students can then easily shuffle or cut and paste paragraphs as they reorganize them for greater coherence. Teacher and peer comments can also be added easily. For second language learners, it is especially important to add comments and questions to their second drafts. This helps these students to expand their pieces with more precise details, and they can do this based on written comments while I circulate and help students who are "stuck." This helps me manage my time efficiently while remaining aware of the process that each student is going through. By the time the final draft is read, which is usually draft four or five, I am intimately aware of each student's writing process.

Chang began by writing the following poem about his grandfather:

When I remember my grandfather, I see his white darkened eyes, filled with blindness. I see his old worn out sweater with stains of coffee on it. I see his old very thin hair, with all the colors washed out.

I hear his old craggy voice which I think it cannot utter a single voice, for it is slowly fading away. I hear his rocking chair as it rubs against the floor. I hear his hum which is as beautiful as the stars and the skies.

I taste his recipes of all kinds of cooking. I taste his candy that he gives me every so often. I taste his authentic oriental cooking that he used to make.

I smell his old clothes that have a color of an uncleaned web filled room. I smell his medicine of some sort which is a smell of a hospital. I smell his bowl of rice which he eats every day.

I touch his smooth skin as it rubs against mine. I touch his bowl of rice for he cannot walk without pain. I touch his old ruined nails which show all the work he has done.

When I remember all these things, he is still alive in my heart.

Notice Chang's attention to detail in this poem, especially his ear for the sounds that create an indelible portrait of his grandfather. Such sensory details come across more eloquently in a poem, yet these sounds remained a major thread in Chang's prose piece. Even in his first prose draft Chang added other details, such as his grandfather's words of advice. In conferencing, I asked him if he could remember any of this advice: exact quotes would enliven his piece and make his grandfather come alive for the reader. I was struck again by the sounds Chang remembered and developed from his original poem. Chang's final draft (Figure 41) shows the fruits of his revision process (see Appendix A for his earlier drafts).

What was originally Chang's second paragraph has become the lead, and he has incorporated the beauty of his grandfather's words into his details. I especially love his sentence, "His words have sharpened my life, from a dull circle into a sparkling diamond." This sentence plays off his grandfather's words: "Life is like an unsharpened rock and I am the carver of that rock." Chang has carved and sharpened this piece of writing into a work of art by carefully choosing his words and crafting his sentences. He has used writing and revision as a way of seeing his grandfather again.

In another class, Karena chose to write about her cousin Kira. By comparison to Chang's, the words with which her poem begins are somewhat scattered:

When I remember my cousin Kira, I see her long, dark hair running down her back, her dark blue eyes staring down at me, her face covered up with make-up.

I hear the clicking her nails make on the kitchen table, the stirring of the wooden spoon as she stirs the cake mix, the sound of the pan being pushed into the oven.

I smell her strong perfume washing over me, the cake we made together in the oven. I smell soapy water as she washes the pans.

I taste the chocolate cake, the frosting on my fingers as I lick them, the little chocolate morsels melting in my mouth.

I touch the wet bowls as I dry them, the soaking dish towel being put away, my cousin's hand taking mine to go outside and play.

When I remember my cousin Kira, I think of the times we hung out and if we can ever do them again.

As Karena worked from her poem to her map, she added many new details while eliminating some that she had incorporated into her poem. Karena's poem is a good example of how students can use

MY GRANDFATHER

I can still hear my grandfather's voice, as he speaks his wise words. My grandfather was wise, but not fully educated. He had many theories about life. Some were out of line, but some were not. His wise words have inspired me. He has told me to never trust anyone else, unless you can trust yourself first. His words have sharpened my life, from a dull circle into a sparkling diamond. His words have taught me all I know about life, how it can be rocky or as smooth as a baby's skin. He had once told me that "Life is like an unsharpened rock and I am the carver of that rock." I can shape it any way I want to. My grandfather has taught me a lot.

When I was a young boy, I would remember sitting on his lap. He would give me a candy and advice. He would tell me about life as a young boy. Growing up in China was very tough. Jobs were very hard to find, the population was growing by the second. He had told me it was hard to move from Hong Kong, China to Vietnam. It was hard in Vietnam, for you had to boil water to be clean so he moved back to Hong Kong. Later, he moved to the United States of America with my mom and my dad. We are still living here. We will probably stay here for a long time. Things are good here, sometimes.

As I remember my grandfather, I can see his vanilla sweater filled with coffee stains, overlapping his black old pants, which are worn out. His white eyes filled with blindness always gave me a scare, wondering what might happen tomorrow. I can still feel the vibration of his old craggy voice, which reminded me of a tuba, deep, deep sweet melody. His very thin hair was the color of grey, like the color of a shiny new metal.

Sometimes I can even see my grandfather rocking in his chair. The screech of the chair would always annoy me, but now that it is gone, I miss it like I miss the hum of his voice, in a sweet melody. The hum would always follow what ever was on the radio. These are some of the things I miss, but what I mostly miss is him.

Figure 41: Final Draft of Chang's Memoir "My Grandfather"

poetry in their rehearsal stage to begin thinking about a topic. Here is the opening paragraph of Karena's first prose draft:

When I was little, my older cousin, Kira, would come over once a week. I remember as she walked into my house the scent of her perfume coming in, grabbing me, and covering me with warmth. She would bend down and look at me with her dark, round eyes and give me a kiss on my cheek with her apple red lips. She would leave a big kiss mark on my cheek. She used to have long Indian necklaces around her neck and I remember always wanting to grab them, but I didn't. I could hear the clicking her bracelets made when she moved her wrists and I loved, absolutely loved her rings. She wore one silver ring on each finger. She had long dark hair running down her back. Most of the time she would put it up in a pony tail. It looked really nice. She usually wore baggy shirts and baggy jeans. Sometimes she would wear a flannel shirt over it.

Notice how much more detail Karena gives here than in her poem about how Kira looked and what she wore. Writing is a way of remembering, and with each revision we dig further back into our memories and retrieve more bits and pieces.

In their early drafts, I noticed that the students repeatedly began paragraphs with pronouns and limited themselves to very simple sentence structure. So I designed my next few mini-lessons to look at literary models to see how authors vary their sentences by combining ideas using adverbial or adjectival phrases and clauses. We also looked at ways to begin sentences with adjectives or prepositional phrases. We read examples side by side with simplified versions that I created for comparison. Sometimes the ears are better editors than the eyes, and it is important to read pieces aloud to know which versions flow better. I urged the students in preparing their next drafts to read their sentences out loud and to experiment with ways to combine or add to them.

I have found, in particular with at-risk students, that these kinds of lessons are crucial in giving them the tools to transition from writing simple, sometimes crude sentences to writing complex, even lyrical ones. The lyric aspect is enhanced for those students who continued to work on writing poetry. The prose writing, in turn, allows them to develop the craft of writing vivid, varied sentences.

These lessons also helped their English teacher to address grammar points that are a required element in the curriculum. Instead of using isolated grammar exercises, grammar instruction was woven into the writing process. For second language learners, this is a particularly effective way to internalize grammatical structures. I also saw from my students' writing that they actually used the mini-lessons to improve their pieces. The special needs educator, who also worked in our class, commented that she could see that the students were gaining confidence in their ability to write and were no longer hesitant when approaching new writing tasks. It is this kind of feedback, reflection, and cooperation among co-teachers that helps students realize their greatest potential.

Students conferred with each other on a daily basis about their progress, often clarifying their meaning or commenting to each other in their native languages. I was eager to capitalize on this interaction, so I had the students engage in "formal" peer conferencing by writing down their suggestions on prepared response sheets. This helped them listen more carefully to each other's pieces and focus their comments. Especially when armed with specific questions to guide their thinking, peers make wonderful writing teachers.

In Karena's third draft, she went on to incorporate both peer suggestions and the mini-lessons about varied sentences to craft more detailed sentences. Notice the more complex structure to her sentences in the following:

I remember the scent of her perfume as she walked into the house, coming in, grabbing me, and in two seconds flat the perfume was covering me with warmth. She would bend down and look at me with her light, oval, blue eyes and give me a kiss on my cheek with her rose pink lips.

Karena's writing was now beginning to flow easily from sentence to sentence and from paragraph to paragraph. In this draft, she also experimented with her conclusion. She wrote:

In this past story, I told you a lot about Kira, what she looked like, how she acted. But I forgot to state one thing. She loved everyone and everyone loved her back. She always cared for people and that is why I loved her so much. We shared many fun times together up until she moved a couple years back and we lost touch with each other. I hope that when I see her again, we can relive our joyful memories and become best friends like we used to be.

This conclusion contains several of the elements that were explained and discussed in our mini-lesson on conclusion writing. We looked at how various authors conclude their pieces and listed five basic strategies that authors use to conclude a piece of writing:

1. Repeat the main idea.
2. Make a recommendation.
3. End with the last event.
4. Use a quotation.
5. Summarize the feelings or qualities of a person.

We decided together that numbers one, four, and five would probably work best with memoirs. This lesson also helped the students to see that an author's conclusion is almost as important as his or her lead, as it is the conclusion that can leave the reader with a lasting impression of the person we are describing (Murray, 1985).

Conferencing with the students about their endings, I asked them what they wanted the reader to remember most about their significant adult: what was it about this person that made him/her special and endearing? Joe answered, "My dad works very hard, but he always finds time to spend with me; he helps me solve my problems." Nathaniel captured his feelings about his grandmother this way:

The whole seven years I knew my nana were some great years. I'll always remember those times I spent with her, like the times I watched and drooled over her making her Christmas sweets, and when she hugged and kissed me on the cheek. Those great Thanksgivings were the days I really remember because everybody's heart was rejoiced with love.

Memoirs have captured many memories for my students and myself, both joyful and painful. As a writing community, we have learned once again the power of words to validate the diversity of our experiences.

CHAPTER 8

La pura vida: Writing Poetry in Spanish with Urban Adolescents—The Link to Developing Academic Spanish

In the poem "Learning English" (Carlson, 1994), a Spanish speaker calls out to us that to truly understand him, he says, "you have to know Spanish, feel it in the blood of your soul" (p. 17). I, too, believe that to understand a person one has to know his or her language. Thus, as a teacher in a city where 85% of my students spoke Spanish as their first language, one of my first priorities was to learn Spanish. Moreover, as a poet, I wanted to share my enthusiasm for Federico García Lorca, Pablo Neruda, and Sandra Cisneros with my students. This would be a sign of respect and a chance to establish common ground.

In learning a new language, I also was able to observe first hand many of the processes that I had studied and apply some of the theoretical insights from graduate courses in second language acquisition. To learn Spanish as quickly as possible, I immersed myself in the oral and written word. I listened to tapes on my one hour daily commute and practiced my "new" words with my students and bilingual colleagues as often as possible. I listened carefully to the nuances of the language to pick up the dialects and accents. As well as reading poetry to increase my vocabulary, I wrote poetry in Spanish using the patterns of language that were inherent in the lines of Neruda and García Lorca. I carried a dictionary with me everywhere, and if I did not know a word, I would ask or "approximate" the word as closely as I could. As I worked side by side with the bilingual teachers, I learned much from them and from their students. Their constant encouragement and appreciation of my efforts gave me further impetus to practice both my written and spoken Spanish. I realized early on how tired my brain became from constantly moving back and forth from English to Spanish, and this helped me to identify with my students who were experiencing the same process in reverse.

Even though I grew up in a bilingual Greek-English household and was fluent in French as a student, learning Spanish at this later age, with my greater understanding of language acquisition, gave me many insights into my students' learning process. I began to realize, however, that in many cases my "literate" or written Spanish was more sophisticated than my students' native speaker speech. Cummins (1984) theory of the common underlying proficiency between two languages convinced me that students who were literate in their own language would make the transition to English with far less difficulty than those who did not have firm native language literacy. I was particularly worried about students who seemed to be illiterate in both Spanish and English. Like other researchers, I had found that many Spanish speaking students had been introduced to only a limited number of strategies when being taught to read and write in their native tongue (Au, 1993; Flores, Cousin, & Diaz, 1991). This knowledge helped me to formulate strategies for working with students to develop their fluency and vocabulary.

In addition, as an "outsider" I could share with my students my genuine excitement over the beauty of the new words that I was learning. Some students were truly surprised when I told them that they were lucky to know two languages and that this was an advantage in our increasingly global society. Moreover, Spanish, with its inherent musicality, is an ideal language for writing poetry. By sharing my poetry with my students, I was able to inspire them to enrich their vocabularies and try new strategies for expressing themselves in both Spanish and English.

Marta and Nelia, the seventh and eighth grade bilingual education classroom teachers, were particularly appreciative of my enthusiasm for Spanish. They commented that I was the first "angla" teacher to attempt to learn and use Spanish with their classes. At first they were openly hesitant about my poetry ideas, but they were willing to invite me into their classrooms. Since both were "traditional" in their style of teaching, using highly structured lessons based directly on textbooks, poetry was a great risk-taking step for them. For me, just opening my mouth to speak in Spanish was a risk. Inwardly, I was terrified that my accent was horrible, that I didn't know enough vocabulary or idioms, and that my ideas would bomb with these street-wise adolescents. My only confidence was in the power of words and in the strength of my enthusiasm for learning.

These classes soon became the highlights of my week. There were twenty-five students in each class, ranging in age from twelve to sixteen. They were predominately from Puerto Rico and the Dominican Republic; many were living with relatives while one or both parents were still in their native countries. It was not uncommon for students to leave in the middle of the year, to move, and then reappear the next year or move to another school within the city. I found that by teaching self-contained poetry lessons that were rich in language I was able to meet some of the literacy needs of my transient students. I also discovered that, in contrast to their very sophisticated and mature appearance, these students embraced poetry with innocence and openness. Moreover, because of their love of music, they could easily identify with metaphor and simile; Spanish love songs are rich in metaphor and dramatic language, and this knowledge was a great way to "hook" my students into the writing of poetry. Tying in an art project with each piece of writing was another tactic that proved successful with almost every class.

Without Marta's and Nelia's assistance, I could never have succeeded as well as I did. They were able to translate and elaborate upon many of my ideas. Another unique advantage that I had was that I always "piloted," as it were, my presentations with Nelia's seventh grade class, and then was able to modify or change the idea completely before I went into Marta's eighth grade class. In that way, we all could share our ideas with each other, so it was, in many ways, like teaching a grade seven and eight combined class; the literacy level in both classes was very similar. In the second and third years, I expanded many of the poetry techniques and began adding more sophistication as my own language expertise improved, and as I discovered more books in Spanish.

Early Classes

"*Buenos días*," I said as I smiled at twenty-five curious eighth graders. I explained in both Spanish and English that I was a writing teacher and that I would be visiting their classes once a week. We would strike a deal: while they helped me with my Spanish, I would help them with their English. I declared, "*Estudio todos los días pero necesito practicar!*" (I study everyday but I need to practice!) I wanted my students to know that I was a curious and involved learner as well as a teacher, and that I would need their help. In beginning this way I hoped to set a tone of community in these classrooms.

In those early weeks, it seemed a good idea to build on my students' experiences living in tropical climates. Since many of them had recently moved to the Northeast, their memories of their native countries were still vivid. After learning about the techniques of showing not telling and using the five senses, we wrote our first poems based on a pattern of remembering using the five senses. The following pattern was written on the board:

Cuando recuerdo mi país,	*When I remember my country,*
veo	*I see*
oigo	*I hear*
huelo	*I smell*
saboreo	*I taste*
toco	*I touch*

We wrote several collaborative examples, with Marta and I both pushing the students to recall specific details. While I explained in English, Marta would translate into Spanish and model the task by recalling specifics from her home in Puerto Rico. Marta's enthusiasm and high expectations for her students to finish a "polished" poem conveyed to these adolescents that this exercise was important. We both conferenced with students, asking them to revise for specifics; for example, if they said "comida," we asked for a specific kind of food. I began learning a lot about *parchas, mangos,* and *arroz con habichuelas* as students described these foods to me. As students sensed my genuine interest, they began to try harder. We looked together in the dictionary for correct spellings and Marta acted as final editor.

One of our first published books was about memories: *"Los recuerdos."* The students wrote fondly about the countries from which they had come. William, an eighth grader, wrote the following poem:

Cuando recuerdo a Puerto Rico
Veo las hojas de los árboles moverse con la brisa
como cuando veo el cabello de una muchacha
oigo a los gallos cantar como oigo que silban las olas del mar
huelo las montañas como huelo el perfume de una muchacha.
saboreo el agua de coco, como saboreo el refresco de china.

When I remember Puerto Rico
I see the leaves of the trees moving with the breeze
like when I see the hair of a young lady
I hear the roosters crowing like the waves of the ocean whistling
I smell the mountains like the perfume of a young woman
I taste the coconut milk like tasting orange soda.

William liked to joke around a lot in class, but poetry and art helped to channel a lot of his energy into creative efforts. His English was quite good, so I drafted him to be my interpreter when I needed help. When the computers arrived in the Writing Center, William began helping me with the typing of poetry in Spanish for our publications. Whenever I could, I identified students who were potential leaders in the classroom and tried to convert them into allies in writing. This strategy helped students like William to shine in a positive way and helped to exert positive peer pressure on those who might not be as willing to write.

We spent several weeks writing about special places, experimenting with different formats, and expanding our use of language. In another class, Jeanilda chose the following format to write about the memory of her special place:

Ven conmigo al campo de Santo Domingo.
Donde puedes ver el río de aguas cristalinas.
Donde puedes oír el cantar de los trinos.
Donde puedes oír el murmullo de la brisa fresca.
Donde puedes tocar las flores llamadas violetas.
Donde puedes tocar el agua fresca.
Donde puedes oler las rosas frescas que se cultivan en mi patria.
Donde puedes oler el perfume de su pureza.
Donde puedes probar las ricas frutas.
Donde puedes probar la sinceridad de mi patria querida,
República Dominicana
es mi lugar especial.

Come with me to the countryside of the Dominican Republic.

Where you can see the crystal clear river.
Where you can see the beautiful butterflies.
Where you can hear the song of the nightingales.
Where you can hear the whisper of the cool breeze.
Where you can touch the cool water.
Where you can smell the fresh roses that grow in my home land.
Where you can smell the perfume of its purity.
Where you can taste the rich fruits.
Where you can taste the sincerity of my dear home land, Dominican Republic.
It is my special place.

In this poem Jeanilda expresses her great love for her native country. I have observed that poems like this one are important for students like Jeanilda to write. As they express their identities by recalling the beauty of their tropical islands, their self-esteem and pride grow. Notice, too, that as students are asked to recall more specific details, they learn to manipulate language and sentence structure in more developed ways.

This poem also demonstrates the author's experimentation with structure. She uses the repeating line opening *Donde puedes…/Where you can…* to introduce things you can see, hear, etc. Poetry can be made accessible to students by pointing out that writing poetry consists of designing patterns with words and sentences; poets can create their own patterns by incorporating a variety of devices, just like Jeanilda does here with parallel structures.

In addition, by helping students to use similes in their writing along with the five senses, I gave them two additional strategies to use in Spanish. Capitalizing on my students' knowledge of Latin music, I asked them to listen carefully for poetic phrases in Spanish songs and to try to incorporate something similar into their own poetry. I also suggested that they write about subjects that were important to them.

As a result of our early work together, each student made a wallpaper book in which all of his or her poems were bound. This was a great accomplishment for us and generated a feeling of pride in the class. Each student read his or her favorite poem in front of the class, and we all clapped. The contrast between the demeanor of these street-wise adolescents and the simple beauty of their poems reinforced my sense of the genuine power of literacy. I also think that these students, perhaps for the first time, felt the impact of becoming part of what Frank Smith calls "the literacy club" (1983).

Nelia's Seventh Grade

After writing about memories, we decided to create a big book in Spanish for Halloween: *Vípsera del Día de brujas.* I was hoping to create a library of Spanish big books that could be shared with the younger grades, thus providing further motivation for writing for an audience; Halloween seemed like a perfect place to begin. We based the book on a poem that expanded the use of the five senses to describe the sights, sounds, and smells of this particular night. Dressed up like a witch, to the excited calls of *¡bruja!* ("witch!") from my students, I shared my poem on chart paper as a model:

Escucha los sonidos del Día de brujas: *La puerta que chilla* *El fantasma que aúlla* *Los niños que ríen.* *Mira los escenarios del Día de brujas* *Los murciélagos que vuelan* *Las brujas que vuelan sobre las escobas.* *Toca* *Los espíritus del Día de brujas* *Los monstruos que espantan a los niños.* *Huele* *Los olores del Día de brujas* *Los dulces chocolates que se derriten en mi boca.* *¡El Día de brujas está aquí!*	*Listen to the sounds of Halloween* *The door that squeaks* *The ghost that howls* *The children that laugh.* *See the scenes of Halloween* *The bats that fly* *The witches that fly on the brooms.* *Touch the spirits of Halloween* *The monsters that frighten the children.* *Smell the smells of Halloween* *The sweet chocolates that melt in my mouth.* *Halloween is here!*

The students then worked in groups divided according to the five senses. They brainstormed possible lines, after which we combined the various lines into parts of the book. In all, the project took four weeks to complete, with Nelia working on the illustrations when I wasn't in class and students working with me in the Publishing Center to finish the writing. Even though we finished in late November, we still had fun sharing our book with the younger grades. Just as in Marta's class, these early published books helped to convey to these students the sense that their language and culture were important and that writing was a cause for celebration. They also began to think of themselves as authors.

Developing Vocabulary and Poetic Technique

New England in the fall is replete with harvest vegetables that are little known to children from tropical climates. Even Marta had never seen gourds in so many sizes and shapes. Living in Concord, which is surrounded by farm stands for much of the year, I took this opportunity to share some of our environment with the students: I loaded my car with huge cornstalks and a basket of pumpkins, gourds, peppers, squashes, apples, cider, pears, asters, bittersweet, colored leaves, and acorns. I also brought into class many pictures and books about the change of seasons. This caused great excitement and curiosity in the classrooms, and we had a lot of fun searching for the words in Spanish to describe our local treasures.

Bringing in these items helped to build my students' background knowledge about both New England and the harvest season. Writing poems in which they took repeated patterns and substituted new vocabulary in each line helped the students develop their poetic technique and facility with language. In this case the repeating line *I am going to pack/ Voy a empaquetar* answered the question "What am I going to pack in a box marked autumn?" Gabriela wrote the following poem in response to this exercise:

¿Qué voy a empaquetar en una caja marcada otoño?

Voy a empaquetar calabazas amarillas como el sol.
Voy a empaquetar los maíces verdes y amarillos como las matas verdes y amarillas.
Voy a empaquetar mucha amistad.
Voy a empaquetar la noche que es oscura como el bosque.
Voy a empaquetar las hojas que caen a la tierra como la lluvia que cae del cielo.

What are you going to pack in a box marked autumn?

I am going to pack squashes that are like the yellow sun.
I am going to pack the corn that is green and yellow like shrubs.
I am going to pack abundant friendship
I am going to pack the night that is dark like the woods.
I am going to pack the leaves that fall on the earth like rain that falls from the sky.

This was one of Gabriela's early poems. I met her for the first time as an eighth grader in Marta's class. She had moved from New York and was living with her aunt. She confided to me early on that she wrote lots of poetry and kept a journal. A quiet, serious student, she was very willing to help her peers with their poems. She also frequently volunteered to read her poems, which helped inspire the class.

Gabriella was unusual in her excellent command of the Spanish language. Most of my bilingual students needed help with the finer points of Spanish grammar and often struggled to find the right words when a task called for a rich descriptive vocabulary. I would often help students find more specific details by looking for words in the dictionary or in the new thesauruses that we had ordered. Their teacher and I circulated among the students, encouraging them to create word pictures with their writing. This became our mode of revising; we did quick revisions with the students, so that they could feel successful and share their final draft at the end of the class period. We felt that this element was important in building academic vocabulary as well as a momentum for a love of writing. As the year progressed, this kind of intervention was needed less and less; at the beginning, however, this format helped my bilingual students feel successful about writing poetry in their heritage language.

Helen, another quiet student, found her voice in the class through her poems. She would rarely read her own poems aloud, but she didn't mind if a friend shared her writing. In February, we wrote versions of Browning's famous poem "How Do I Love Thee?" Helen's poem illustrates her use of similes and the progression of her language from our early attempts in the fall:

¿Que cómo te quiero?
Te diré de cuantas maneras.
Te quiero como la luz del sol brillando sobre la tierra.
Te quiero como las flores en primavera.
Te quiero como el cantar de los pájaros temprano en la mañana.
Te quiero como la lluvia que cae del cielo a la tierra.
Te quiero como los colores del alba.
Te quiero como un beso en mi alma.
Te quiero como la brisa del campo.

> *How do I love you?*
> *Let me count the ways.*
> *I love you like the sunlight shining over the earth.*
> *I love you like the flowers in the spring.*
> *I love you like the song of the birds early in the morning.*
> *I love you like the rain that falls from the sky to the earth..*
> *I love you like a kiss in my soul.*
> *I love you like the country breeze.*

Notice the beauty of the images "kiss in my soul" and the "song of the birds in the early morning." Notice also how Helen combines similar consonant sounds in phrases like "sunlight shining" and "falls from the sky." She is beginning to choose words for their musicality. These are just some of the elements that teachers can use to assess students' language development through their writing of poetry.

Using Picture Books as Jumping Off Points

Sometimes I would begin a poetry lesson by reading a folktale in Spanish that was particularly evocative of unusual language or events. One such book is *Moon Rope: Un lazo a la luna* by Lois Ehlert (1992), which I found in our local library. This Peruvian folktale, stunningly illustrated in a manner that recalls pre-Columbian artwork, is a whimsical tale of a fox and a mole and their attempts to reach the moon. One goal of reading this book was to emphasize to students the rich variety of cultures within the Latino world. Another was to capitalize on the book's beautiful language and extensive use of the subjunctive mood in Spanish, which would open up whole new possibilities for writing poetry. Dwelling on the wishes in the story, I suggested that the students think of their most unusual wishes and write a kind of "list poem" describing them. The following is the model that I wrote:

> *Yo quisiera una flor que cante en la lluvia.*
> *Yo quisiera una luna que brille de día.*
> *Yo quisiera ir al mar más profundo para darle la mano a un pulpo.*
> *Yo quisiera ir al cielo para poder volar con los pájaros.*
> *Yo quisiera ir bajo la tierra para escuchar a las flores mientras florecen.*

> *I would like a flower that sings in the rain.*
> *I would like a moon that shines in the day.*
> *I would like to go to the deepest sea to shake hands with an octopus.*
> *I would like to go to the sky so I can fly with the birds.*
> *I would like to go inside the earth in order to listen to the flowers growing.*

I emphasized to the students that in this poem they could let their imaginations soar with wishes that were impossible to attain in reality, but possible to attain through the magic of poetry. Jessica, a seventh grader, wrote the following poem in response:

> *Yo quisiera tener un gato que me hable día y noche.*
> *Yo quisiera ir al océano y hablar con los peces.*
> *Yo quisiera ir al cielo de noche para ver las hermosas estrellas.*
> *Yo quisiera ser un arco iris para brillar todos los días.*
> *Yo quisiera ser una sirena para estar todo el día en el agua.*

> *I would like to have a cat that talks to me day and night.*
> *I would like to go to the ocean and talk with the fish.*
> *I would like to go to the sky at night to see the beautiful stars.*
> *I would like to be a rainbow in order to shine every day.*
> *I would like to be a mermaid in order to be in the water every day.*

Thanks to federal grant money, I was able to order a series of bilingual folktales available from Children's Press, which allowed us to explore additional permutations of this exercise. I also got the class a subscription to *Listo,* Scholastic's news magazine of events in the Latino World. These were ways to connect my students to the Latino world, with its wealth of diverse customs. Even within our own "world," there were differences in customs and vocabulary between students from Puerto Rico and the Dominican Republic. This helped us all to realize the richness of our cultures

Encouraging Fluency: Playing with Words

While building vocabulary through books, magazines, and songs, I continued to use poetry as a way to expand and enrich my students' fluency. Listing things that are beautiful, silent, etc. is another poetic technique for encouraging the expansion of ideas. Examples of this poetic tradition can be found in the works of Gertrude Stein, Paul Simon ("Fifty Ways to Leave Your Lover"), F.Scott Fitzgerald, John Cheever, and Pablo Neruda. As poets, the way we play with the juxtaposition of words makes the poem at once musical and evocative. In that vein, we had fun making list poems in Spanish of *cosas que son hermosas* ("things that are beautiful") and *cosas que son silenciosas* ("things that are silent"). Students enjoyed elaborating upon these lists and inventing their own. After they wrote their final drafts, I laminated their poems into cards. This is a simple strategy that I often used to show students that all their writing was important.

Color poetry is another format that encourages fluency because of its word associations. First, we go around the room naming things that are yellow, for example. Students invariably name such things as *ropa* (clothes), *lápiz* (pencil), *muro* (wall)—things that can be dyed any color. This leads to a lively discussion of things that are naturally colorful—*cosas que son de la naturaleza* (things that are from nature). These discussions often last as long as twenty-five minutes, but I have found them essential in helping students find the images that they need when they are searching for comparisons from which to construct similes. Eve Merriam's poem "A Yell for Yellow" (1962) is a poem filled with images of yellow and is a rhythmic poem to read aloud to follow up these discussions. Because I knew that most of my students had a fairly good understanding of English, and that this understanding must precede written and oral competence in the language, I often interspersed English poems with the Spanish ones. Following this lesson, Carola, an eighth grader wrote this poem about her favorite color, turquoise:

> *Coloréame de turquesa, como el hermoso Océano Pacífico.*
> *Coloréame de turquesa como la brillante piedra aguamarina recién nacida.*
> *Coloréame de turquesa como el más importante de los colores translúcidos.*
> *Coloréame de turquesa como la sirena que se pasea por todas las costas.*
> *Coloréame de turquesa como los sinceros y puros ojos de un niño.*
> *Coloréame de turquesa como la perla de una ostra del mar más profundo.*
> *Coloréame de turquesa como el barco que va sin rumbo.*
> *Coloréame de turquesa porque de todos los bellos colores, él es el más hermoso.*

> *Color me turquoise like the beautiful Pacific Ocean.*
> *Color me turquoise like the shiny aquamarine stone that has just been born.*
> *Color me turquoise like the most important of the translucent colors.*
> *Color me turquoise like the mermaid that passes by every coast.*
> *Color me turquoise like the sincere and pure eyes of a child.*
> *Color me turquoise like an oyster pearl from the deepest sea.*
> *Color me turquoise like the sailing ship that goes without direction.*
> *Color me turquoise because of all the beautiful colors, it is the most beautiful.*

As is common with translations, Carola's poem loses some of its beauty in English. In Spanish the sounds flow like the ocean that she is writing about. Notice also how she has tied together all her images relating to the sea. Carola, an eighth grader, had a sophisticated command of the Spanish language. When she wrote, her pencil just flowed over the page, pouring out word after word. Her revisions involved minor word or punctuation changes. She was also a talented artist, and she spent a great deal of time perfecting the artwork she wanted to accompany her final drafts. As with all lessons such as these, students at many levels of development can benefit from expanding their word choice or finding unusual combinations of words in the way Carola did in this poem.

In addition to formal poetry lessons, we often started class with word games that would encourage divergent thinking and help students think in metaphors. For example, one of my favorite games is to name a shape, like round, and then go around the room asking each student to come up with something that is round: *redondo como el sol, como el globo, como la luna llena* ("round like the sun, like the globe, like the full moon"). In this exercise I challenge students to think of unlikely comparisons; to think like a poet is make comparisons that add another dimension to our thinking.

Poco a poco: Como una tortuga
I often commented to my principal that I was making progress in my Spanish like a turtle—little by little. For the students, I could see progress over time, especially when I was lucky enough to work with students in Spanish for two years in a row. The great lessons I learned were patience and appreciation for the difficulty and risk-taking that change entails.

Dolly is an example of a student with whom I worked for two years. In sixth grade, she worked diligently in writing but had difficulty with the manipulation of language, partly because she had a limited vocabulary in both Spanish and English. She hardly ever wavered from any pattern that I introduced and rarely volunteered to read her poems. Early in seventh grade, however, she began taking small risks in writing. The following is one of her early poems:

> *Cuando recuerdo a Puerto Rico*
> *Veo las olas del mar como si viera a mi madre.*
> *Oigo el viento como si oyera las olas de mar.*
> *Huelo las flores que huelen como el perfume de mi madre.*
> *Saboreo las frutas de Puerto Rico y los cocos frescos.*
> *Toco la bandera de Puerto Rico como si tocara la piel de mi madre.*

> *When I remember Puerto Rico*
> *I see the waves of the sea as if I were seeing my mother.*
> *I hear the wind as if I hear the waves of the sea.*
> *I smell the flowers that are like my mother's perfume.*
> *I taste the fruits of Puerto Rico and the fresh coconuts.*
> *I touch the Puerto Rican flag as if I were touching the skin of my mother.*

In this poem Dolly is experimenting with the sounds of words but hasn't stretched her vocabulary to include specific details or strong images. However, I am moved by the nostalgia she feels for her island home and her mother. She is taking a step here toward writing with a more personal voice.

Later that year, Dolly began taking more risks in writing; she had absorbed and was using many of the poetic techniques that had been introduced. They were finally making sense to her and she was able to make independent use of them in her writing. One gorgeous spring day, I suggested to the students that they address spring lovingly, in appreciation for all its gifts; poetically, we could even embrace, hug, kiss, or envelop spring in our arms. Dolly surprised me by using all these terms of endearment in her poem to spring. She varied each line, playing with the verbs that could envelop her in spring:

> *Primavera, acaríciame con tus suaves manos.*
> *Bésame con tus labios carnosos.*
> *Cántame como el sol que alumbra la mañana.*
> *Abrázame con tus fuertes brazos.*
> *Coloréame como el color de las flores.*
> *Báilame como la salsa de Puerto Rico.*
> *Mójame con la lluvia que cae por la noche.*
> *Alúmbrame con la luz de tu corazón.*

> *Spring, caress me with your soft hands.*
> *Kiss me with your great lips.*
> *Sing to me like the sun lights the morning.*
> *Hug me with your strong arms.*
> *Color me like the color of the flowers.*
> *Dance with me like the salsa of Puerto Rico.*
> *Wet me with the rain that falls in the night.*
> *Light me with the light of your heart.*

Asignar nombres
Another technique that I used with success to develop metaphor in writing is what I call "Namings" or *"Asignar nombres."* We were inspired by the García Lorca poem, *"Noche"* (Night), (1955) which assigns to the night such unusual names as "candle," "lamp," "lantern," and "firefly."

First, we discussed Lorca's unusual names for night and I encouraged the students to think of unusual names for common things that they see around them everyday. Stressing to them that poetry is the act of making the ordinary extraordinary, I asked them to think of the qualities of these things or to focus on the relationship of the object to other things near it. For example, the sea could be named the home of whales, the road for ships, the gift of mermaids, or the mirror for clouds. As we went around the room naming things, students began to choose their topics. The following poem by Leonel is particularly evocative:

La luna	*The Moon*
La risa de la noche.	*The smile of night.*
La vecina del sol.	*Sun's neighbor.*
La cara que nos mira en la noche.	*The face that sees us at night.*
La novia de la noche.	*Night's fianceé.*
La prima de las estrellas.	*The stars' cousin.*

This deceptively simple poem requires complex higher order thinking skills. It also stretches students' capabilities for writing metaphor and painting word pictures. These poems lend themselves to art, and the students made beautiful cards to showcase their poems and drawings. We put up a display in the library to celebrate our work. Displaying the students' writing in Spanish throughout the school let everyone know that this was a language to be proud of. This was another way to publish students' writing. Often, oddly enough, even though our school was made up of a student population that was 85% Latino, the bilingual classes were considered quite separate from the mainstream classes; I found that through writing and publishing we were able to come closer together in our accomplishments.

Odas

Pablo Neruda's poetry inspired us all to write odes. An ode often glorifies its subject using lofty language; it is a poem of praise. The poems I read to introduce odes were almost exclusively by Neruda. In his *Odas elementales* (Odes to Simple Things), Neruda (1958) wrote poems of praise to hundreds of things, from watermelons to shoes, socks, storms, etc. In these poems he transforms the ordinary into the extraordinary, showing us that poetry can make us see the wonders that are all around us.

Because of the sheer beauty of his use of language, I found that Neruda could help us all to become better writers. Due to our lack of poetry books in Spanish, I often assembled handout packets of poems by one or more particular poets, so we could study their words more closely. I found these packets and our work with them to be the most effective tools in helping students to absorb words and emulate technique. This method was also my subtle way of helping teachers to rely less on texts and more on their own choices of literature.

Through this experience, odes became one of my favorite teaching forms. Through odes, students can develop their use of metaphor and personification to a sophisticated level. Moreover, celebrating Neruda, the Nobel Prize winning Chilean poet, let students know that, yes, there are talented and famous Latino and Latina authors.

Before writing our own poems we read Neruda's "*Oda al limón*" (Ode to Lemon) out loud. Here, Neruda addresses the lemon as though its very essence had transformed his soul. After reading this poem, I asked the students to choose something that they felt passionate about, something that had transformed their lives. They were to begin the poem by addressing the object and to follow this with lines that glorify all its wonderful qualities. In the following ode to night, Karla, a seventh grader, celebrates the peace and beauty of night:

Noche, viniste sola en el aire como una guitarra voladora llena de brisa que me acariciaba en la noche. Los grandes ojos me miraban desde la ventana. Llegaste oscura y desolada como la capa del día. siempre alumbrada por pequeñas estrellas brillantes. Las flores bailaban con tu pequeña brisa y tu hermosa luna brillante me acompañaba en mis sueños.	Night, you came alone in the air like a flying guitar full of breezes that caressed me in the night. The great eyes watched me from the window. You came with small tears that refreshed nature. Night, you came dark and desolate like the cape of the day always illuminated by small bright stars. The flowers danced with your small breeze and your beautiful, bright moon came with me in my dream.

Notice how carefully Karla chose the images for her ode; it is almost a lullaby that soothes our senses to sleep. In contrast, Aliana, another seventh grader, celebrated the exuberance of nature in her ode to spring:

Oda a la primavera Primavera llegaste con flores y con luz me llenaste con tu calor y ternura tu belleza alumbró mi alma me arropaste con tus cálidas alas. Primavera llegaste con alegría y esperanzas viniste con dulzura y olor a rosas me llenaste con tu sonrisa tierna viniste como algodón y absorbiste el frío y la tristeza que existían en mí.	Spring, you arrived with flowers and with light. You filled me with your warmth and tenderness. Your beauty illumined my soul. You clothed me with your wings of warmth. Spring, you arrived with joy and hopes. You came with sweetness and smell of roses. You filled me with your tender smile. You came like cotton and you absorbed the cold and the sadness that existed in me.

Notice the way Aliana ends her poem with the image of cotton absorbing the coldness and sadness of winter. This is a very sophisticated idea and makes the warmth of spring even more apparent in her poem!

As this example shows, form can inspire students to crystallize their thoughts; it can also liberate them to write about their deepest feelings. Sometimes they would write odes to sadness, to their mother or aunt, to the Virgin Mary, or to their boyfriends. I was touched by the number of odes written to mothers; through these odes I discovered the importance of family and relationships to my bilingual adolescents; urban adolescents, in particular, combine unusual maturity with a sensitivity to language that enables them to write poetry that startles with both its beauty and its emotions.

Playing With Rhyme

As I became more experienced myself in reading and writing Spanish, I was able to try more daring ideas. For example, García Lorca's poem, *"Vals en las Ramas"* inspired me because of its fanciful images and its rhyme scheme. This poem delves into the surreal imagination of the mind. I discussed with students, too, the work of artists like Dalí, Magritte, Kahlo, and De Chirico, who explored surrealism through their paintings; I brought into class reproductions of paintings that explore images in unusual ways and urged students to explore unusual scenes in their poems. I asked them to imagine something falling, like in Lorca's poem, and then to imagine a series of events that happened as a result of the object falling. If they wanted to try a rhyme scheme similar to Lorca's, they could also add rhyme to their poem as an additional challenge.

The following poem by Gabriella is especially wonderful:

Vals de la rosa	*Waltz of the Rose*
Cayó una rosa	*A rose fell*
y dos	*and two*
y tres.	*and three.*
Por el viento volaba un cangrejo	*A crab flew though the wind*
y el cielo estaba bien.	*and the sky was well.*
Los ojos de la pequeña niña	*The little girl's eyes*
lagrimeaban	*teared*
y yo estaba en cama;	*and I was on the bed;*
ella buscó la luz del cielo	*she looked for the light of the sky*
y yo también la busqué	*and I also looked for it*
porque cayó una rosa	*because a rose fell*
y dos	*and two*
y tres.	*and three.*
Por eso me puse triste y lloré	*Because of this, I became sad and cried*
y una planta hecha de papel	*and a plant was made of paper*
y un caballo comió miel	*and a horse ate honey*
y la mosca lo miró a él.	*and the fly looked at him.*
Uno por uno	*One by one*
dos por dos	*two by two*
tres por tres	*three by three*
¡Oh piedra de madera!	*Oh, stone made of wood!*
¡Oh casa de papel!	*Oh, house made of paper!*
con el zumbido de las abejas,	*with the roar of the bees*
con el quiquiriquí del gallo,	*with the crow of the rooster*
y el miau del gato.	*and the meow of the cat.*
Llegará una vaca gorda	*A fat cow will arrive*
condenada a muerte.	*condemned to death.*
¿Será el viento tan fuerte	*Will the wind be as hard*
como el huracán?	*as the hurricane?*
Andrés irá muriendo con él.	*Andrés will go on dying with him.*
Uno a uno	*One to one*
como la Cumbia	*just like a cumbia (dance)*
dos por dos	*two by two*
alrededor de la terraza	*around the porch*
y tres por tres	*and three by three*
y podrán moverse las paredes.	*so the walls can move.*

Notice the rhymes that Gabriela chose, like *papel* (paper) with *miel* (honey) and *él* (him). She also incorporated internal rhyme in her line *"oh piedra de madera"* ("oh, stone of wood"). Gabriela, a talented poet, chose her images for their startling qualities. On her writing survey, Gabriela confirmed what she had told me earlier in the year: that writing poetry was her favorite kind of writing. She answered, too, that Federico Pizarro was her favorite writer because she liked the way he expressed himself in his poems. She was definitely connecting her reading to her writing.

Gabriela wrote many love poems, too. The following poem exemplifies the passion that went into her work:

Te extraño

Te extraño como los pájaros extrañan la primavera
Como los árboles extrañan al otoño
Como la nieve extraña al invierno
y como se extraña a un amor verdadero.

Te extraño como los peces extrañan la libertad
Y el arco iris extraña sus colores
que colorean todo a su alrededor
para que brille de felicidad.

Te extraño como se extraña la felicidad que en tus brazos no puedo
reemplazar.

Con todas estas palabras
te extraño y quiero que regreses ya
porque no puedo vivir con tanta crueldad.

I miss you like the birds miss the spring
like the trees miss autumn
like the snow misses winter
and like one misses a true love.

I miss you like the fish miss liberty
and the rainbow misses its colors that will color everything around it
so that it shines with happiness.

I miss you like the happiness that in your arms
I cannot replace.

With all these words
I miss you and want you to come back now
because I cannot live with so much cruelty.

When Gabriela had an opportunity to work with our musician in residence, who we hired through an arts grant, her lyrical poetry soared into a love song that swept our school with its popularity. *"Como te amo"* is a classic love song with a *merengue* beat:

Te amo
como los pájaros
aman la libertad.

Te amo
como al aire puro
que respiro.

Te amo
como las olas
aman el mar,

y como el anochecer
ama la soledad,
y la tranquilidad en el desierto.

Así te amo yo,
así te amo yo,
como la noche
a la tranquilidad.

Así te amo yo
como los pájaros
a la libertad.

Así te amo yo
como la noche
a la tranquilidad.

Así te amo yo
como los pájaros
a la libertad.

In working with the musician in residence, Gabriela was very clear as to the kind of music she envisioned for her words. This kind of collaboration was a natural outgrowth of our work in writing that year, and through it the students could easily see and hear the beauty of their native Spanish. When Gabriela's song was performed at our annual Writing Conference, students began clamoring for copies of the cassette that we produced. Her song also made our school recognize that our bilingual students had many gifts to share and that they were indeed an integral part of the school community. I spent many hours dubbing tapes of these songs by Gabriela, Rosangela, Elana, and Moises. They became our local celebrities!

The Story Continues

I continue to study Spanish on my own by listening to tapes, reading poetry and picture books, and translating the lyrics to music that I buy. I practice speaking to my daughter, who is minoring in Spanish in college, and to my bilingual colleagues at school. Whenever I need cheering up, I phone Marta; she just came back from visiting Mexico City and was filled with enthusiasm for all that she saw. She keeps in touch with our students, and I have found out that many of the students mentioned in this chapter have moved either to another state or back to Puerto Rico. Marta told me recently that she keeps a photo album of all her students and that when she looks at their pictures she can remember the poems that they wrote. Poetry has impacted her life as a teacher. In a formal evaluation, she wrote: "It's been wonderful to see how our students—who at the beginning thought that writing poems was out of this world for them—have changed their minds.... [I]t improves the kids' self-esteem [to] see what they're capable of."

I believe strongly that students need to be literate in their heritage languages. Not only did I notice that these students' self-esteem improved as they became more literate in Spanish, but I observed how easily my literate seventh grade students adjusted to being mainstreamed into eighth grade

English classes; they easily transferred the poetic techniques that they learned in Spanish to their writing in English. Along with my students, I, too, grew tremendously through my knowledge of another language during this time. Our mutual gifts had the power to change us all.

CHAPTER 9

Student Writing Conference: A Celebration of Poetry and Music

In the spring, as a way to celebrate student writing, we staged a Writing Conference with a festive atmosphere at which students could attend master classes and then write and perform their poetry and music. This event established a model that I believe could be emulated at other schools.

Getting Started

To set up a Writing Conference, a school first needs one or more business partners and funding to invite poets and/or musicians to lead master classes. We found that the local Arts Lottery and the district Education Foundation were good sources of grants for this purpose. As far as business partners, our administrative team established partnerships with local newspapers and with a local college, which provided a suitable venue at which the conference could be held.

Once these elements are in place, teachers nominate a number of students to participate in the conference based on their passion for writing, whereupon the nominees are asked to submit poems. Then a committee and a designated chairperson select the best poems. In our case, about ninety students from grades 6-8 were selected to attend the conference. The committee then creates a shortlist of themes or techniques that a particular set of poems might suggest and submits them to a poet or musician, who is thus able to work out a program for Writing Conference day based on the students' own material.

Preparing for the Conference

Before the conference, a group from the conference committee fill the Writing Conference Folders with the following: a Writing Conference Button, writing paper, pens and pencils, a "My Name Is" sticker, and the conference program. These folders are then arranged alphabetically in three different boxes by grade level. Students are also encouraged to bring their journals and to write in them in Spanish, English or other native languages.

Another important element in the preparations is printing the invitations for the conference, which also serve as permission slips. The selected students are invited to an assembly and given the invitations as well as information on the Writing Conference. Meanwhile, committee members work on inviting community guests and district personnel to sit at tables of ten students and collaborate with them on their writing. In our case, we arranged for as many teachers to attend the conference as possible, in some cases through the hiring of substitutes and in some cases by having teachers attend on a rotating schedule during their free blocks.

Another key element in making this event special is to make sure students attend the conference dressed as much like professionals as possible—no tee shirts or jeans! When students enter the lobby of the conference facility, teachers hand them their folders, which have been sorted by grade and have numbers on the front. The numbers indicate tables to which the students have been randomly assigned, thus ensuring a diverse group of students working together at each table.

Celebration

On the day of the Writing Conference, students are called to the auditorium to go over the rules. Then they are escorted to the conference site in waves by grade level, which allows the handing out of folders to flow in an organized manner. After they pick up their folders they proceed into the

For You, the Writer

You write beautifully.
Don't stay silent too long.
Don't turn into
A follower.

Come out of your shell.
And don't be afraid to do what you do
  best.
Write about the trees,
The moon
The earth
And the mountains.

Don't forget how
You might be alone.
Walk around.
Sit by yourself.

And don't forget to write.

Figure 42: Conference Poem: "For You, the Writer"

conference area and find their numbered tables.

The program begins with one or more master classes by the invited artists, who blend poetry and song into their presentations. Students then work in their groups to write poems based on the techniques and music they have heard or to create their own unique poems in English or other languages. Students also translate their work into English with the help of the native language teachers. This is usually a time of tremendous excitement, creativity, and collaboration. Students are encouraged to write poems collaboratively and then to perform their poems together. This kind of collaboration affirms our status as a community of writers. Teachers and artists also circulate around to the various tables to help students find the right words or the music to accompany their poems.

By the time the writing is finished, students are so excited about performing their poetry that very little encouragement is needed when they are asked to come to the microphone to do so. This is the high point of the conference. In this phase, students are called to the podium table by table. Alone, in pairs, or in small groups, they celebrate their identities through their writing as their peers cheer them on.

My Voice

My voice is a light to the world.
Cutting like a knife through the dark
  of the world.
My voice is an alarm clock of the
  world.
Waking people up to the problems that
  must be solved.
My voice is a rainbow of colors over
  the world.
Showing there is more than one color.
My voice is a ray of sun shining on
  the world.
Warming the world with the warmth
  of love.
My voice sounds loud, and it will be
  felt.

Figure 43: Conference Poem: "My Voice"

Let It Out

Speaking out is something we all need
  to do,
About prejudice, religion, justice, even
  you.
All around the world, people are not
  doing so,
Look for people everywhere, both high
  and low.
Let it out, let it out! Say what you
  want to say,
Not next year, not next month, not
  tomorrow, but today!
See, isn't it better that you got it off
  your mind,
Teach people to do the same, find as
  many as you can find.
You don't have to be embarrassed, you
  don't have to be afraid.
Tell your friends, anybody, about how
  they've behaved.
Let it out, let it out! Say what you
  want to say,
Not next year, not next month, not
  tomorrow, but today!

Figure 44: Conference Poem: "Let it Out"

Publishing the Memories

When the performance session ends and before the catered lunch begins, we ask students to pass in the final draft of their poems so we can type them for inclusion in an anthology of poetry from the Conference. This becomes yet another way to trace the growth of students' writing toward sophisticated poetry and music. Figures 42 through 44 show a sampling of poems on human justice, which was the theme of our third annual conference. As you read these poems, think about how strong they are in their voice and vision. These students now see the power of words—the power of literacy to change not only themselves but also the world.

Finally, Figure 45 shows a checklist that teachers and administrators can follow when planning their school's own writing conference:

Pre-Festival/Organizing the Events

Student Component	Teacher/Admin./Artist Component
1. Once they have been nominated, students are asked to submit poems. This is done at least one month to six weeks before the festival. 2. Selected students are invited to an assembly where they are given their invitations/permission slips. A one-week deadline is given for returning the signed permission slips.	1. A grant is written one year ahead for the artists involved in the conference. 2. Administration establishes a business partnership and a contact person. 3. The Writing Conference Chair sends a memo to the faculty, asking for volunteers to form a Writing Conference Committee. 4. The Committee sends out nomination papers to each grade level team. A two-week deadline is given for returns. 5. The Committee selects final poems and sends twenty or so to the artists for inclusion in the program. 6. Chair and artists contact each other to discuss the theme and prepare the conference program. 7. A sub-committee sends out invitations to the conference to community and district leaders. 8. Coverage is arranged by the administration for teachers to attend the conference. 9. Invitations are printed for the selected students. 10. Teachers accompany students to an assembly where they are given their invitations and permission slips. 11. The Conference Committee meets to stuff folders with buttons, writing paper, pencils, "My Name Is" labels, and the conference program. Numbers are randomly assigned from 1-10 to indicate table seating (10 students per table) and student names are affixed to labels on folders.

The Writing Conference

Student Component	Teacher/Admin./Artist Component
1. At 8:30 AM the selected students are asked to come to the auditorium. Rules of the conference are reviewed, whereupon students are divided by grade levels. 2. Accompanied by teachers, students proceed to the conference site. 3. Students pick up their Conference Folders and find their assigned tables.	1. Teachers meet students in the lobby of the conference site, where they are given conference folders. (8:15 AM) 2. The Chair and the principal open the Writing Conference with a few words of congratulations to the students; then the artists are introduced. (8:45 AM) 3. Master Class(es) by the artists, who have incorporated student work into the program. (9-10 AM) 4. Students write their poems and songs. (10-11 AM) 5. Students perform their poems and songs. (11 AM-12 PM) 6. Before lunch, students are asked to pass in their poems to the Chair to be published in a Conference Anthology. 7. Lunch of sandwiches and soda for students, artists, teachers, district and community guests, and Committee members. (12-1 PM) 8. Students are escorted back to school to attend their remaining classes. (1 PM)

Post-Festival

	Teacher/Admin./Artist Component
	1. Teams are asked to type their students' poems and save them on discs in similar font and format. This is expected to take a few days to complete. Discs are then given to the contact person from the business partnership to compile and publish as a poetry anthology to be given to students before the end of the school year.

Figure 45: Writing Conference Checklist

CHAPTER 10

Making Connections to the Content Areas

Poetry is a powerful tool for connecting English language learners to grade level content area concepts and materials. As they read in the content areas, students begin to expand and develop their academic English. In a study by Worthy, Ivey, and Broaddus, (2001), students reported that having the right materials motivated them to read. Content area literacy depends on a growing knowledge of specific and sophisticated vocabulary as well as the application of research skills to writing. Thus, poetry can provide an ideal motivator for expanding vocabulary and expanding concepts.

Figure 46: Social Studies Poem "Queen Nefertiti"

For example, Social Studies is a natural context to connect students to cultural concepts and sophisticated vocabulary. Here, poetry makes history come alive for students and helps them to internalize concepts. In a sixth grade unit on Egypt, we discovered the many Egyptian gods through the art of poetry. Students were given a vocabulary bank with descriptions of the gods, which they turned into short poems enlivened by Egyptian style art (Figures 46-49). A simple form that begin-

Figure 47: Social Studies Poem "Pharaoh"

ning English language learners can use for such poems is the *cinquin,* which works as follows:

Noun (name of god)
Two adjectives describing the god
Three –*ing* verbs describing what the god does
Four words giving a definition of the god
Fifth line is a one-word name for the god.

After looking at the information packet of vocabulary words and descriptions of the gods, Daphne declared, "This is easy." She wrote the following poem:

Hateshput
Beautiful, great
Inventing, reigning, changing
The greatest Egyptian ruler
Queen

Figure 48: Social Studies Poem "Hieroglyphs"

Another sixth grader wrote the following poem about King Tut:

King Tut
Young, rich
Ordering, telling, guarding
A good loved person
Ruler.

Jennifer was fascinated by the goddess Osiris and wrote the following:

Osiris
Dead, Green
Willing, Excepting, Ruling
A husband of Isis
Mummy.

These poems show the students not only developing their English by using parts of speech but exploring their word banks for words that make their god meaningful to them. A more sophisticated form for students to try is based on a famous hymn from ancient Egypt. The hymn is introduced to

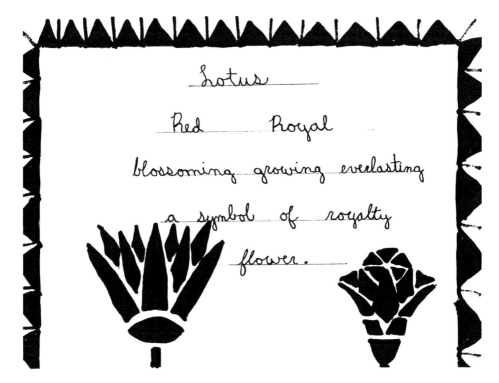

Figure 49: Social Studies Poem "Lotus"

students by explaining that hymns of praise were an important part of Egyptian culture. The following ancient Egyptian hymn is then put on an overhead:

O Beauteous one
O Beauteous one, O cow, O great one,
O great magician, O splendid lady, O queen of gods!
The King reveres you, Pharaoh, give that he live!

Behold him, Hathor, mistress from heaven
See him, Hathor, mistress, from lightland,
Hear him, flaming one, from ocean!
Behold him, queen of gods, from sky, from earth,
From Nubia, from Libya, from Manu, from Bakhu,
From each land, from each place, where your majesty shines!

Behold what is his inmost,
Though his mouth speaks not;
His heart is straight, his inmost open,
No darkness is in his breast!
He reveres you, O queen of gods,
Give that he live!

After sharing this hymn with students I encourage them to think of a god to sing praises to using this poem as a model for basic structure.

In ancient Egypt, a hymn could also be addressed to an important symbol. I demonstrate this approach using the following poem, which I write on the overhead while talking through the process so students can see how I compose my lines:

Hymn to the Sun

Oh, sun, bright fiery orange one,

Giver of light and life
Giver of warmth and food
Oh, sun, round, hot one
Giver of thirst and drought
Without you, we couldn't see
Without you, we couldn't live
Oh, sun, you take my breath away.

After students see these two examples, I encourage them to choose either a god or a symbol that represented Egypt and to sing its praises in a hymn. This poetry writing exercise incorporates their new content knowledge about Egypt, specifically about the various gods and the important symbols that archaeology tells us represent ancient Egyptian life. The students write their final drafts in cartouches and decorate them with Egyptian symbols.

Matt wrote the following hymn to Hathor:

Oh, Hathor, Cow headed Hathor
Giver of music and love
Give me love and happiness.
Oh, Hathor, mighty Hathor
Giver of women and children
Without you there would be no happiness
Oh, Hathor, Goddess Hathor
Without you evil would rule.

As students shared their ideas while they were writing and chatting, poems began to pop up all over the room. Students were also sharing their collective knowledge about ancient Egypt, thus adding to their storehouse of knowledge. This kind of collaboration inspires students to find words of their own and to further research the background knowledge required for their content areas. Following this process, another sixth grader wrote the following poem:

Ode to Anubis

Oh, Anubis, embalmer of the dead
Why must you be so powerful?
Anubis, it is you that helps bring people beyond death into the new world.
Oh, riser of the dead, who is to embalm you when you're ready to begin your new life?
Anubis, why must you have the head of a jackal and not of a human?
Oh, powerful one, you are the one I have worshiped.

Another way poetry can be used to connect students with social studies is through the study of historical events. Recently, teachers have used poetry to tap into the affective realm of history learning (Kane & Rule, 2004). Similarly, in an eighth grade unit on the study of the Holocaust, students in advanced ESL classes were reading a play about Anne Frank. To complement this reading and to enter the affective realm of history, I used the bilingual book *Dear Anne Frank* by the Chilean poet Marjorie Agosín (1998). The poems in this volume, in Spanish and English, are written in an address format, in which the poet addresses Anne Frank with many questions such as adolescents would have about her life in hiding. We discussed both the imagery and the content of the poem as students read along in their own packets. I have found that these poems genuinely touch students' lives while connecting them to a crucial period of history.

The following poem is a result of this lesson. The students were asked to write first in Spanish, as this unit raised such emotional issues that it was easier for them to express themselves in their native language first. Later, we worked on translating the poems into English:

Querida Ana Frank

Cuéntame
Ana Frank,
Tú crees que Dios es justo haciéndote esto a ti y a miles de personas que
Mueren sin saber el ¿por qué?
Detrás de estas cuatro paredes tus días se consumen
Tu niñez va quedando
Atrás y son muy pocas las cosas que puedes hacer.
Sabes
Hoy afuera el sol brilla,
Los pájaros vuelan,
Y las mariposas se posan de flor en flor.
Ellos no saben que tú estás encerrada en una pequeña jaula día y noche.
Quizás,
Si lo supieran vendrían hasta aquí, para hacer tus días más felices.

¿Tú piensas que el monstruo de la guerra terminará algún día?
Yo pienso que sí y espero que este día llegue pronto
Y tú puedas contar esto en tu sueños.
¿Cuál es tu sueño?
Sueña, Ana,
Por que el soñar es ser libre
Pero tú
¡Tú no eres libre!

> *Guadalupe*

Dear Anne Frank

Tell me,
Anne Frank
Do you believe that God is just making you and millions of others die without knowing why?
Behind these four walls your days are consumed
Your youth stays behind as well as the many things you would like to do.

Do you know
Today that outside the sun shines
The birds fly
And the butterflies alight from flower to flower.
They do not know that you are hidden in a small jail day and night.
Perhaps,
If they could visit you here, your days would be much happier.

Do you think that the monster of the war will end each day?
I think that if I believe that this day will come soon and
You could sing this in your dreams.
What is your dream?
Dream, Anne,
Because to dream is to be free

But you
You are not free!

The incredible beauty of this poem lies in its emotional attachment to the reality of Anne Frank's life and its acknowledgement of the horrors of war and anti-Semitism. For second language learners, to write this in their first language connects them to the essence of history in a way that allows them to ultimately manipulate ideas in two languages and make the ideas their own. This kind of empathy establishes a deeper level of understanding about the Holocaust than memorization of statistics and place names can ever do. It demonstrates an internalization of the realities of World War II for the many Jews and others who lived in daily terror of being taken away to concentration camps and worked, tortured, or simply put to death.

Science is another content area that is especially suitable for poetry due to the fact that both poets and scientists are observers. Moreover, the language of science is often metaphorical in order to render abstract concepts in an understandable way. Thus, poetry can help to deepen students' knowledge of both science concepts and vocabulary. In a sixth grade unit on astronomy, for example, we found many poetry models with which students enjoyed working. The poem "Thirteen Ways of Looking at a Blackbird" by Wallace Stevens (1990), for example, can be used to introduce the idea of looking at something very closely and in many different ways. Preparing a criteria chart beforehand also helps guide students' expectations for the final product in a scientific way. The following criteria chart (Figure 50) was developed to give students guidance in their writing:

Category	Choices/Suggestions
Format	**Choose One:** • Riddle poem • Persona Poem: "I am…" • Found poem: words from magazines or science articles • Acrostic poem • Thirteen ways to look at…
Science Content	**Include:** • Five specific details • Five related facts (ten line minimum)
Figurative Language	**Use:** • Metaphor • Simile • Personification
Rhythm	**Use:** • Repeating line(s) • Repeating sound(s)
Word Choice	**Select:** • Vivid verbs • Specific nouns • Exciting adjectives
Mechanics	**Final Draft/Edit for:** • Spelling • Punctuation

Figure 50: Criteria Chart for Science Poem

With these guidelines in mind, students were shown the following models on the overhead:

Personification
Song of the Stars

We are the stars which sing.
We shine brightly.
We are the ones who give light at night.
We fly through the sky.
We are many.
We make constellations.
We are different sizes.
We are sharp and rounded.
We are of the galaxy Milky Way.
We are awake day and night.
We are the stars which sing.

Persona Poem
Song of the Sun

I am the sun.
I have many rays.
I shine brightly in the morning.
I give you light in the day.
I see many comets whizzing by.
I am the center of your universe.
I am the closest star.
I am the sun.

Riddle Poem
I am the planet nearest the sun.
I am 93 million miles from the sun.
I have two small moons and ice caps at the poles.
I am surrounded by broad rings which revolve at different speeds about my equator.
I am the furthest planet that rotates like a top that is spinning on its side.
I am one of the twin planets.
I am the most recently discovered planet.
I have 24 hours in my day.
I have a red spot on me that changes in brightness from time to time.
About three-fourths of my surface is covered with bright reddish or yellowish patches.
I am the brightest body in the sky next to the sun and moon because my thick clouds reflect so much sunlight.

These three models demonstrate how the use of such poetic devices as metaphor, persona, and personification can add another dimension to the study of science.

CHAPTER 11

Conclusion: Poetry, High Stakes Assessment, and Standards Based Instruction

It has been my experience that in both urban and diverse suburban areas, writing instruction that is based on poetry and vocabulary building improves students' scores on state assessment tests. In one urban area, our students gained steadily over a three-year period, outscoring all other city schools and showing the greatest improvement in reading and writing. In a diverse suburban area, our English language learner population consistently came through the ELA MCAS exam with a 90% passing rate.

For the ELA MCAS Open Response questions, students must be prepared to analyze at least three poems over the course of three sessions. In connection with Maya Angelou's poem "Caged Bird" (1986), for example, students might be asked the following question: "What conditions of the human spirit do the 'caged bird' and the 'free bird' represent? Explain your answer using detailed evidence from the poem." Before reading the poem, students should read the question to determine what they need to know and what text to underline as evidence for their answer. This is a good opportunity to go over vocabulary, underline phrases, and brainstorm for various "conditions of the human spirit," such as freedom, slavery, hope, happiness, peace, liberty, and love.

To aid students in structuring their analyses, I provide them with the following chart (Figure 51), which we fill in together on the overhead:

Symbol	What it represents	Evidence from the Text	Line or Lines
Free bird	Freedom	Free bird	Line 1
Cage	Slavery	Cage	Line 8
Bars of rage	Anger	Bars of rage	Line 10
Sings of freedom	Hope	Names the sky his own	Line 21
Names the sky his own	Ownership, freedom	Leaps on the back of the wind; thinks of another summer breeze	Line 1 (free bird)
		Sings with a fearful trill	Line 14

Figure 51: Chart for Poetry Analysis

Students are encouraged to scan the poem for further evidence to weave into their responses. After providing students with the topic sentence "The caged bird and the free bird represent opposite conditions of the human spirit," I ask them to write their responses using the information on the chart found or other textual evidence. The following two samples are from ESL IV seventh graders' practice responses:

The caged birds and the free bird represent opposite conditions of the human spirit. The caged bird represents slavery in contrast the free bird represents freedom.

In lines 11-12, the poet says that his wings are clipped and his feet are tied. I believe that the poet shows that the caged bird represents slavery because the slaves are just like the caged bird (they have no freedom at all).

In lines 4-6, the poet says the he dips his wing in the orange sun rays and dares to claim the sky. I believe that the poem shows the free bird represents freedom because it sounds like it's his own sky (just for him and nobody else's).

This answer demonstrates how students use the chart to provide a basic structure but go deeper into the poem to find additional lines that are meaningful to them. Comparison to the following shows how students use different supporting evidence to support their opinions:

The caged bird and the free bird represent opposite conditions of the human spirit. The caged bird represents slavery. In contrast the free bird represents freedom. I believe the poet is showing that the cage bird is representing slavery because in line eight, the caged bird stalks down in its narrow cage. I believe this because slaves were caged in too. In contrast, the free bird represents freedom. The poet shows the free bird representing freedom in line twenty-one. In line twenty-one the poet talks about how the free bird thinks of another breeze. This in my opinion shows that the bird shows the human spirit of freedom and liberty. This is how the caged bird and the free bird represent the human spirit.

Poetry can serve as the foundation for many other kinds of writing. For second language learners, it builds academic language skills both in English and in native languages in unique and powerful ways. Moreover, in content areas such as social studies and science, poetry can provide added motivation to learn new vocabulary and concepts and can help students to develop a personal relationship to their new knowledge base. Content areas require research, reading and writing as well as grasping new information. Poetry can help students become better readers and can accelerate their writing in addition to their vocabulary development. Research, in turn, comes more naturally to students who are motivated to read and write and who feel confident in their abilities in these areas. Thus, poetry based writing instruction can make major contributions to the middle school curriculum while helping young adolescents come to terms with their own languages, identities, and roles as readers, writers, and members of a community.

APPENDIX A

Chang's Drafts of His Memoir "My Grandfather"

My Grandfather

When I was a young boy I would rember sitting on his lap. He er would give me candy and tell of his wise words. He would tell me about life as a young boy. Growing up in China was very tough, jobs were very hard to find, the population was growing by the second. He had told me it was very hard to move from Hong Kong, China to Vietnam. It was hard in vietnam, for you had to boil water in order to clean. But he finally settled in Hong Kong, China those are some of the good and bad things.

Draft 1

My Grandfather

My grandfather was wise, but not fully educated. He had many theorys about life. Some ~~words~~ were out of line. But some were not. His wise words had inspired me. ~~He has~~ told me that to never trust anyone else, unless you can trust yourself first. His words have shapened my life, from a dull circle into a sparkling diamond. His words had taught me that all I know about Life.

These are great details. Can you remember any other advice?

Draft 2

My Grandfather

3

When I remember my grandfather I see his *nannila* sweater filled with coffee stains, overlapping his black old pants which ~~has been~~ ~~worn~~ *are worn* out. His white eyes filled with blindness, always gave me a scare, wondering what might happen tomorrow. I can feel the vibration of his old deep craggy voice, which reminded me of a tuba, its deep-deep ~~and~~ sweet *with* melody. His very thin hair ~~which~~ is the color of grey, like the color of a shiny new metal. — *great details*

Draft 3

My Grandfather

(4)

I can see my grandfather rocking in his chair. The screech of the chair would always annoy me, but now that it is gone, I miss it, like I miss the hum of his voice is a sweet melody. The hum would follow the same tune as whatever was on the radio. These are some of the fun things that I miss. But what I mostly miss is him.

lovely!

Draft 4

APPENDIX B

Evaluation Materials

3. Blank Writing Survey (English)

Student Writing Survey

This survey will help us to know you better as writers. It will tell us about your interests in writing and what you think good writers do. Please answer the questions as completely as you can. Thanks for your help!

Name _____ Date _____ Grade _____

1. What kinds of things do you write at home? Who helps you?

2. What kinds of things do you write in school? Who helps you?

3. What do you like to write about?

4. How do you choose what to write about?

5. What is your favorite kind of writing? Poetry? Fiction? Essay or report? Other?

6. When you write a story or report, how do you get ready to write?

7. When you come to a word you can't write or spell, what do you do?

8. When you finish writing, what do you do?

9. If a young child asked you how to write, what would you tell him/her to do?

10. What do you think the steps are in writing a book?

11. What is good writing?

12. What do you think good writers do?

13. Have you even written a story or book you were proud of?

14. What was the topic? Why do you think that was your best writing?

15. Who is your favorite writer/author? Why?

3. Blank Writing Survey (Spanish)

Encuesta Sobre las Obras Escritas de los Estudiantes

Esta encuesta nos permitirá conocerlos mejor como escritores. Nos dirá sobre tu interés por escribir, y lo que piensas que hacen los buenos escritores. Por favor, contesta las siguientes preguntas, de manera tan completa como te sea posible. Gracias por tu ayuda.

Nombre _____ Fecha _____ Grado ____

1. ¿Qué clase de cosas escribes en tu casa? ¿Quién te ayuda?

2. ¿Qué clase de cosas escribes en la escuela? ¿Quién te ayuda?

3. ¿Sobre qué cosas te gusta escribir?

4. ¿Cómo escoges los temas sobre los que escribes?

5. Cuál es tu estilo favorito para escribir?

6. Cuando escribes una historia o un informe, ¿cómo te preparas para escribir?

7. Cuando hay una palabra que no sabes cómo se escribe o cómo se deletrea, ¿qué haces?

8. Cuando terminas de escribir, ¿qué haces?

9. Si un niño pequeño te preguntara cómo se escribe, ¿qué le contestarías?

10. ¿Cuáles crees que son los pasos que se deben seguir para escribir un libro?

11. ¿Qué es para ti la buena escritura?

12. ¿Qué crees que hacen los grandes escritores?

13. ¿Alguna vez has escrito una historia o un libro del que estuvieras orgulloso? ¿Cuál era el tema?

14. ¿Crees que ese fue tu mejor trabajo escrito? De ser así, ¿por qué?

15. ¿Quién es tu autor o escritor favorito? ¿Por qué?

---

4. Growth Self-Evaluation, Sixth to Eighth Grade

How have I grown in writing from grade six to grade eight?

It took three years for me to learn to write as well as I do. When I first began writing I couldn't even write one line that didn't seem plain. Now each line I write has meaning and depth. My details used to be flat and simple but I soon learned many captivating words to use in the place of ordinary ones.

My best writing now is mostly poems, but I hope someday I will write a novel. Sometimes it takes me a while to choose a topic and a style of writing but when I finally do, my writing just takes off. I often wonder how I can keep up with the pen gliding across the paper.

I like to think of how lucky I am to have gotten the opportunity to become a great writer. When I think of how I've improved so far I can only begin to imagine where my writing will take me in the future.

Mrs. Bearse has taught me the fun in writing in all subjects. She has shown me both serious and fun ways to write about nature or the issues we face today. In everything I write I get a chance to express both feelings and ideas.

Completed Writing Survey (6th grade)

STUDENT WRITING SURVEY

This survey will help us to know you better as writers. It will tell us about your interests in writing and what you think good writers do. Please answer the questions as completely as you can. Thanks for your help.

Mrs. Bearse

Student
Name. ....Date.............................
Grade...6...Room.........................

1. What kinds of things do you write at home? Who helps you?

Homework and letters wich my mom or dad help sometimes.

2. What kinds of things do you write in school? Who helps you?

School work and no one helps except once in a while.

3. What do you like to write about?

A lot of different things.

4. How do you choose what to write about?

I write about the first thing that comes into my mind.

5. What is your favorite kind of writing? Poetry? Fiction? Essay or report? Other? I'm not to good at writing poetry but I lik tow rite poetry an Essays.

6. When you write a story or report, how do you get ready to write?

I sharpen my pencil and get a clean piece of paper.

7. When you come to a word you can't write or spell, what do you do?

I look it up in the dictionary if it's not there I ask for help.

8. When you finish writing, what do you do?

I reread it and fix mistakes.

9. If a young child asked you how to write, what would you tell him/her to do?

I would start with letters a, b and c and show them how to write them.

10. What do you think the steps are in writing a book?

Prewriting, rereading, rewriting, editoring, and final draft.

11. What is good writing?

Good writing is putting effort into it.

12. What do you think good writers do?

I think good writers think before they writ.

13. Have you ever written a story or book you were proud of?

Yes, I have written many short storys Ic proud of.

14. What was the topic? And why do you think that was your best writing?

Fall. I think it was my best writing because I put a lot of thinking a effort into it.

15. Who is your favorite writer/author? Why?

Donald J. Sobol because I like the books he wrote I thought they were interesting.

Completed Writing Survey (8th grade)
STUDENT WRITING SURVEY

This survey will help us to know you better as writers. It will tell us about your interests in writing and what you think good writers do. Please answer the questions as completely as you can. Thanks for your help.

Student
Name...Date...
Grade.....8..Room...

1. What kinds of things do you write at home? Who helps you?

Sometimes poems or letters but also compositions for school. Noone.

2. What kinds of things do you write in school? Who helps you?

Poems, short stories, memoirs, and book reports. The teachers mostly Mrs. Bearse.

3. What do you like to write about?

Everything ranging from nature to issues like violence and crime.

4. How do you choose what to write about?

It depends on the day and how I feel. If it is a nice day and I am happy I will write about somethi cheert

5. What is your favorite kind of writing? Poetry? Fiction? Essay or report? Other?

Poetry. That is what I write most.

6. When you write a story or report, how do you get ready to write?

First, I find a clean quiet place to work then I think about the topic for awhile and figure out a wa everything in neat

7. When you come to a word you can't write or spell, what do you do?

I look it up in the dictionary.

The Sky in My Hands: Accelerating Academic English through the Writing Process

8. When you finish writing, what do you do?

I reread my work to make sure it is satisfactory.

9. If a young child asked you how to write, what would you tell him/her to do?

I would ~~tell~~ tell him/her to find a topic that interests them then write what they feel about it, but it is more complicated than just that.

10. What do you think the steps are in writing a book?

First you need a story line, then you must extend your ideas and do a lot of revisions. Then you need to have it edited. Finally you have to write the final draft.

11. What is good writing?

Good writing is writing that the writer is satisfied with.

12. What do you think good writers do?

What every writer does only better and they are recognized for it.

13. Have you ever written a story or book you were proud of?

I've written a memoir and was very proud of the result.

14. What was the topic? And why do you think that was your best writing?

It was ~~about~~ about my third grade teacher. It was not my best. My writing is all the best.

15. Who is your favorite writer/author? Why?

I don't have one. I like a variety of authors and cannot choose only one.

REFERENCES

Adamé, L. (1973). My grandmother would rock quietly and hum. In O. Salinas & L. Faderman (Eds.). *The barrio: A Chicano anthology.* New York: Harper & Row.

Agosín, M. (1998). *Dear Anne Frank: Poems.* Hanover and London: Brandeis University Press.

Anaya, R. (1983). Abuelo. In R. Cohen, N. Millett, & R. Rodrigues (Eds.), *Explorations in literature* (pp. 234-237). Glenview, IL: Scott Foresman & Co.

Angelou, M. (1969). *I know why the caged bird sings.* New York: Bantam.

Angelou, M. (1986). *Poems.* New York: Bantam.

Angelou, M. (1993). *Life doesn't frighten me.* With paintings by Jean-Michel Basquiat. New York: Stewart, Tabori, & Chang.

Asher, S. (1989). *Wild words! How to train them to tell stories.* New York: Walker & Company.

Atwell, N. (1990). *Coming to know: Writing to learn in the intermediate grades.* Portsmouth, NH: Heinemann.

Au, K. (1993). *Literacy instruction in multicultural settings.* Oliver, FL: Harcourt Brace.

Baylor, B. (1986). *I'm in charge of celebrations.* New York: Charles Scribner's Sons.

Baylor, B. (1991). *Your own best secret place.* New York: Atheneum.

Bearse, C. (1997). Singing with the words: Using Neruda and Lorca with middle school students. In *Luna, luna: Creative writing ideas from Spanish, Latin American and Latino literature.* New York: Teachers & Writers Collaborative.

Bearse, C. (1998). Ana: Finding a writer's voice. *Currents in Literacy, 1,* No. 1. Cambridge, MA: The Hood Children's Literacy Project, Lesley College.

Bearse, C. (2003). *Identity formation and collaborative inquiry in the zone of proximal development: Grade 8 ESL students doing research—A teacher research study.* Ann Arbor, MI: Pro-Quest.

Bearse, C. I. (1992, May). The fairy tale connection in children's stories: Cinderella meets Sleeping Beauty. *The Reading Teacher, 45*(9), 688-695.

Belitt, B. (Ed.), (1961). *Selected poems of Pablo Neruda: A bi-lingual edition.* New York: Grove Weidenfeld.

Braided Lives: An anthology of multicultural American writing. (1991). St. Paul, MI: Minnesota Humanities Commission.

Burnett, F. H. (1998). *The secret garden.* New York: Harper Trophy.

Calkins, L. M. (1991). *Living between the lines.* Portsmouth, NH: Heinemann.

Calkins, L. M. (1994). *The art of teaching writing: New edition.* Portsmouth, NH: Heinemann.

Carle, E. (Ed.), (1989). *Animals, animals.* New York: Philomel Books.

Carlson, L. (Ed.), (1994). *Cool salsa: Bilingual poems on growing up Latino in the United States.* New York: Henry Holt & Co.

Chavez, C. (1997). A curriculum discourse for achieving equity: Implications for teachers when engaged with Latina and Latino students. Prepared for the Hispanic Dropout Project, January, 1997: Washington, DC. Retrieved July 27, 002 from the World Wide Web: http://www.ncbe.gwu.edu/miscpubs/hdp/3/index.html.

Christensen, L.M. (1991, April). Poetry: Reinventing the past, rehearsing the future. *English Journal,* 27-33.

Cisneros, S. (1989). *The house on Mango Street.* New York: Vintage.

Cisneros, S. (1991). *Woman hollering creek.* New York: Vintage.

Cisneros, S. (1994). Abuelito who. In L. Carlson (Ed.), *Cool salsa: Bilingual poems on growing up in the United States* (p. 55). New York: Ballantine Books.

Clifton, L. (1987). *Good woman: Poems and a memoir, 1969-1980.* Brockport, NY: BOA Editions, Ltd.

Cockburn, V. & Steinbergh, J. (1991). *Where I come from: Songs and poems from many cultures.* Boston: Talking Stone Press.

Collier, V. (1995). Acquiring a second language for school. *Directions in Language & Education 1*(4). Washington, DC: The National Clearinghouse for Bilingual Education.

Collier, J., & Collier, C. (1974). *My brother Sam is dead.* New York: Scholastic Books.

Crichton, M. (1990). *Jurassic park.* New York: Random House.

Cumming, A. (1998). Theoretical perspectives on writing. *Annual Review of Applied Linguistics, 18*, 61-78.

Cummins, J. (1984). *Bilingualism and special education: Issues in assessment and pedagogy.* Clevedon, UK: Multilingual Matters.

Cummins, J. (1996). *Negotiating identities: Education for empowerment in a diverse society.* Ontario, CA: CABE.

Dahl, R. (2000). *James and the giant peach.* New York: Puffin Books.

De Felix, J., Waxman, H. & Paige, S. (1993). Instructional processes in secondary bilingual classrooms. *Proceedings of the Third National Research Symposium on Limited English Proficiency Issues: Focus on Middle and High School Issues.* Washington, DC: United States Department of Education. Retrieved July 16, 2001 from the World Wide Web. http//www.ncbe.gwu.edu/ncbepubs/symposia/third/deflix.html.

Delpit, L. (1991). A Conversation with Lisa Delpit. *Language Arts, 68*, 541-547.

Dunning, S. & Stafford, W. (1992). *Getting the knack.* Urbana, IL: National Council of Teachers of English.

Dyson, A. H. (1989). *Multiple lives of child writers: Friends learning to write.* New York: Teachers College Press.

Ehlert, L. (1992). *Moon rope: Un lazo a la luna.* New York: Harcourt, Brace, & Janovich.

Ekoomiak, N. (1992). *Arctic memories.* New York: Henry Holt & Co.

Emig, J. (1971). *The composing process of twelfth graders.* Urbana , IL: National Council of Teachers of English.

Erickson, E. H. (1968). *Identity, youth and crisis.* New York: W.W. Norton & Co., Inc.

Faltis, C. J. (1999). Creating a new history. In C. J. Faltis & P. Wolfe (Eds.), *So much to say: Adolescents, bilingualism, and ESL in the secondary school* (pp. 1-9). New York: Teachers College Press.

Field, R. (1926). City rain. In S.C. Gross (Ed.), *Every child's book of verse* (p. 63). New York: Franklin Watts, Inc.

Fleischman, P. (1985). *I am phoenix: Poems in two voices.* New York: Harper & Row.

Fleischman, P. (1988). *Joyful noise: Poems in two voices.* New York: Harper & Row.

Flores, B., Cousin, P., & Diaz, E. (1991). Transforming deficit myths about learning, language, and culture. *Language Arts, 68,* 369-379.

Fox, M. (1988). *Koala Lou.* San Diego, CA: Voyager Books.

Fox, M. (1989). *Wilfred Gordon McDonald Partridge.* Brooklyn, NY: Kane/Miller Book Publishers.

Freeman, Y.S. & Freeman, D.E. (2002). *Closing the achievement gap.* Portsmouth, NH: Heinemann.

Garcia, E. (1993). Project Theme: Collaboration for school improvement at the middle school for language minority students, *Proceedings of the Third National Research Symposium on Limited English Proficient Issues: Focus on Middle and High School Issues*: Washington, DC: United States Department of Education. Retrieved July 17, 2001 from the World Wide Web: http://www.ncbepubs/symposia/third/garcia.html.

García Lorca, F. (1993). *Canciones y poemas para niños* (17th ed.). San Juan, PR: Labor Bolsillo Juvenil.

García Lorca, F. & Allen, D. (Eds.), (1955). *The selected poems of García Lorca.* New York: New Directions.

Gee, J. (1989). What is literacy? *Journal of Education 171*(1), 19-25.

Giovanni, N. (1973). *Ego-tripping and other poems for young people.* New York: Lawrence Hill & Co.

Glenn, M. (1982). *Class dismissed!* New York: Clarion Books.

Glenn, M. (1986). *Class dismissed II.* New York: Clarion Books.

Goldberg, N. (1993). *Long quiet highway.* New York: Bantam.

Goodman, Y. M. & Goodman, K. S. (1990). Vygotsky in a whole-language perspective. In L.C. Moll (Ed.), *Vygotsky and education.* New York: Cambridge University Press.

Graves, D. H. (1983). *Writing: Teachers and children at work.* Portsmouth, NH: Heinemann.

Greenfield, E. (1978). *Honey, I love.* New York: Harper Trophy.

Greenfield, E. (1989). *Nathaniel talking.* New York: Black Butterfly Children's Books.

Gutierrez, K. D. (1992). A comparison of instructional contexts in writing process classrooms with Latino children. *Education and Urban Society, 24*(2), 244-262.

Hansberry, L. (1994). *Raisin in the sun.* New York: Vintage.

Hasen, J. (1987). *When writers read.* Portsmouth, NH: Heinemann.

Herschfelder, A. B., & Singer, B. K. (Eds.), (1992). *Rising voices.* New York: Charles Scribner's Sons.

Hidalgo, N. (1992). *"I saw puerto rico once": A review of the literature on Puerto Rican families and school achievement in the U.S.* Report No. 12. Washington, DC: Center on Families, Communities, Schools, and Children's Learning.

Hoffman, M. (1991). *Amazing grace.* New York: Dial.

Holman, F. (1993). *Secret City, U.S.A.* New York: Demco Media.

Houston, G. (1992). *My great-aunt Arizona.* New York: Harper Trophy.

Hoyt-Goldsmith, D. (1992). *Arctic hunter.* New York: Holiday House.

Hudelson, S. (1988). Writing in a second language. *Annual Review of Applied Linguistics, 9,* 210-222.

Huerta-Macias, A. (1998). Learning for Latinos: the sociocultural perspective. In M. Gonzalez, A. Huerta-Macias, & J. Tinajero (Eds.), *Educating Latino students: A guide to successful practice.* Lancaster, PA: Technomic.

Hughes, L. (1995). *The collected poems of Langston Hughes.* (A. Rampersad, Ed.). New York: Vintage Books.

Janeczko, P. B. (1990). *The place my words are looking: What poets say about and through their work.* New York: Simon and Schuster.

Jiménez, R. T., & Gersten, R. (1999). Lessons and dilemmas derived from the literacy instruction of two Latina/o teachers. *American Educational Research Journal, 36*(2), 265-301.

Johnson, A. (1993). *Toning the sweep.* New York: Scholastic.

Johnson, G. D. (1989). Your world. In M. Honey (Ed.). *Shadowed dreams: Women's poetry of the Harlem Renaissance.* New Brunswick, NJ: Rutgers University Press. (Original work published 1922).

Kane, S., & Rule, A. C. (2004). Poetry connections can enhance content area learning. *Journal of Adolescent Literacy, 47*(8), 658-669.

Kendall, R. (1991). *Eskimo boy: Life in an Inupiak Eskimo village.* New York: Sholastic Books.

Koch, K., & Farrell, K. (1985). *Talking to the sun.* New York: Holt, Rinehart & Winston.

Lasky, K. (1992). *Think like an eagle.* Boston: Little Brown & Co.

Ledoux, D. (1993). *Turning memories into memoirs.* Lubin Falls, ME: Soleil Press.

Lewis, R. (Ed.), (1966). *Miracles: Poems by children of the English-speaking world.* New York: Simon & Schuster.

Lewis, R. (Ed.), (1971). *I breathe a new song.* New York: Simon & Schuster.

El libro de la escritura. (1989). New York: Teachers & Writers Collaborative.

Little, J. (1987). *Hey, world, here I am!* New York: Harper & Row.

Lloyd, P. (1987). *How writers write.* Melbourne, Australia: Thomas Nelson.

Lockwood, A. & Secada, W. (2000). *Transforming education for Hispanic youth: Exemplary practices, programs, and schools.* Resource Collection Series, 12, March, 2000. Washington, DC: National Clearinghouse for Bilingual Education.

Lucas, T. (1993). Secondary schooling for students becoming bilingual: Issues and practices. In M.B. Arias & A. Casanova (Eds.), *Bilingual education: Politics, research and practice* (pp. 113-143). Chicago: National Society for the Study of Education.

Machin, N. (Ed.). (1978). *African poetry for schools, book 1.* Essex, UK: Longman Group, LTD.

Markus, H. & Kitayama, S. (1991). Culture and the self: Implications for cognition, emotion, and motivation. *Psychological Review 98,* 222-248.

McKim, E. & Steinbergh, J. (1992). *Beyond words: Writing poems with children* (2nd ed.). Brookline, MA: Talking Stone Press.

McLaine, K. (1986). The writing development of high school secondary language learners in the context of a holistic English as a second language classroom. Unpublished dissertation, Boston University, Boston, MA.

Mercado, C. (1993). Crossing cultural boundaries to learn from and contribute to practice in multiethnic urban settings. *Proceedings of the Third National Research Symposium on limited English Proficient Issues: Focus on Middle and High School Issues*: Washington, DC: United States Department of Education. Retrieved July 17, 2001 from The World Wide Web: http://www.ncbe.gwu.edu.ncbepubs/symposia/third/mercado.html.

Mercado, C. & Moll, L. C. (2000). Student agency through collaborative research in Puerto Rican communities. In S. Nieto (Ed.), *Puerto Rican students in U.S. schools.* Mahwah, NJ: Lawrence Erlbaum.

Merriam, E. (1962). *There is no rhyme for silver.* New York: Atheneum.

Mohr, N. (1979). *Felita.* New York: The Dial Press.

Murray, D. (1985). *A writer teaches writing* (2nd ed.). Boston: Houghton Mifflin.

Murray, D. (1990). *Shoptalk: Learning to write with writers.* Portsmouth, NH: Heinemann.

Myers, W. D. (1988). *Scorpions.* New York: Harper Keypoint.

Myers, W. D. (1993). *Brown angels.* New York: Harper Collins.

Neruda, P. (1958). *Odas elementales.* Buenos Aires: Losada.

Neruda, P. (1986). *Love sonnets: Cien sonetos de amor.* (S. Tapscott, Trans.). Austin, TX: University of Texas Press.

Neruda, P., & Vallejo, C. (1971). *Selected poems, translated by Robert Bly & others.* Boston: Beacon Press.

Nevarez-La Torre, A. (1999). Developing voice: Teacher research in bilingual classrooms. *Bilingual Research Journal, 23* (4), 451-70.

Newman, D., Griffin, P., & Cole, M. (1989). *The construction zone.* Cambridge: Cambridge University Press.

Nieto, S. (1994). Lessons from students on creating a chance to dream. *Harvard Educational Review, 64*(4), 392-426.

Nieto, S. (1999). *The light in their eyes: Creating multicultural learning communities.* New York: Multicultural Education Series.

Noboa, J., Jr. (1987). Identity. In E. Farrell, R. Cohen, & L. J. Christensen (Eds.), *Discoveries in literature* (p. 148). Glenview, IL: Scott Foresman.

O'Neill, M. (1961). *Hailstones and halibut bones.* New York: Doubleday.

Ortiz, S. (1974). I know that feeling. *Yardbird, Vol. 3.* Yardbird Publishing Co., Inc.

Padgett, R. (Ed.), (1987). *The teachers and writers handbook of poetic forms.* New York: Teachers & Writers Collaborative.

Paulsen, G. (1987). *Dogsong.* New York: Puffin Books.

Paulsen, G. (1989). *The winter room.* New York: Dell Publishing.

Peyton, J. K. (1990). Dialogue journal writing and the acquisition of English grammatical morphology. In J.K. Peyton (Ed.), *Students and teachers writing together: Perspectives on journal writing.* Alexandria, VA: TESOL.

Plath, S. (1960). *The colossus and other poems.* New York: Alfred A. Knopf, Inc.

Pomeroy, T. (1987). Making potica. In M. Spring & E. Angeles (Eds.), *Scholastic literature anthologies: Relationships* (pp. 62-63). New York: Scholastic Books.

Prelutsky, J. (Ed.). (2000). *The Random House book of poetry for children.* New York: Random House.

Reyes, M. (1991). A process approach to literature using dialogue journals and literature logs with second language learners. *Research in the Teaching of English, 25*(3), 291-313.

Reyes, M. (1992). Challenging venerable assumptions: Literacy instruction for linguistically different students. *Harvard Educational Review, 62* (4), 427-446.

Ringgold, F. (1996). *Tar beach.* New York: Dragonfly Books

Rising voices: The writings of young Native Americans. (1992). Selected by A.B. Hirschfelder & B.R. Singer. New York: Scribner's & Sons.

Romo, H. D. & Falbo, T. (1996). *Latino high school graduation: Defying the odds.* Austin, Texas: University of Texas Press.

Rong, X. L. & Preissle, J. (1997). *Educating immigrant students: What we need to know to meet the challenges.* Thousand Oaks, CA: Corwin Press.

Rose, M. (1989). *Lives on the boundary.* New York: Free Press.

Rosenblatt, L. (1978). *The reader, the text, the poem.* Carbondale, IL: Southern Illinois University Press.

Rosenblatt (1985). The transactional theory of the literary work: Implications for research. In C.R. Cooper (Ed.), *Researching response to literature and the teaching of English* (pp. 33-53). Norwood, NJ: Ablex.

Rylant, C. (1992). *Missing May.* New York: Orchard Books.

Saunders, W. E., O'Brien, G., Lennon, D., & McLean, J. (1999). *Successful transition into mainstream English: Effective strategies for studying literature.* Santa Cruz, CA: Center for Research in Education, Diversity, and Excellence.

Shange, N. (1993). *I live in dancing.* With paintings by Romare Bearden. New York: Stewart, Tabori, & Chang.

Smith, F. (1983). Reading like a writer. *Language Arts, 60,* 558-567.

Smith, F. (1988). Joining the literacy club. Portsmouth, NH: Heinemann.

Smith, R. K. (1984). *The war with grandpa.* New York: Bantam.

Soto, G. (1991). *A fire in my hands: A book of poems.* New York: Scholastic Books.

Soto, G. (2000). Two dreamers. In *Baseball in April and other stories* (pp. 23-32). Orlando, Florida: Harcourt Brace.

Stegner, W. (1987). *Crossing to safety.* New York: Penguin Books.

Stevens, W. (1990). Thirteen ways of looking at a blackbird. In *Collected poems of Wallace Stevens.* New York: Vintage.

Taylor, M. (1984). *Roll of thunder, hear my cry.* New York: Bantam.

Taylor, M. (1990). *Mississippi bridge.* New York: Dial Books.

Taylor, M. (1992). *The road to Memphis.* New York: Puffin Books.

Taylor, M. (1998). *The friendship.* New York: Puffin Books.

Torres-Guzmán, M. & Thorne, Y. (2000). Puerto Rican/Latino student: Stand and deliver. In S. Nieto (Ed.), *Puerto Rican students in U.S. schools.* Mahwah, NJ: Lawrence Erlbaum Associates.

U.S. Bureau of the Census (1990). *Current population reports: School enrollment.* Washington, DC: U.S. Government Printing Office.

U.S. Bureau of the Census (1993). *Current population reports: School enrollment.* Washington, DC: U.S. Government Printing Office.

Valdés, G. (1999). Incipient bilingualism and the development of English language writing abilities in the secondary school. In C. Faltis & P. Wolfe (Eds.), *So Much to say: Adolescents, bilingualism, & ESL in the secondary school.* New York: Teachers College Press.

Valdés, G. (2001). *Learning and not learning English: Latino students in American schools.* New York: Teachers College Press.

Van Manen, M. (1990). *Researching lived experience.* Albany, NY: State University of New York Press.

Viorst, J. (1972). *Alexander and the terrible, horrible, no good, very bad day.* New York: Aladdin Paperbacks.

Viorst, J. (1984). *If I were in charge of the world and other worries: Poems for children and their parents.* New York: Aladdin Paperbacks.

Voices from the future. (1993). Children's Express. (Ed. S. Goodwillie). New York: Crown Publishers.

Voigt, C. (1981). *Homecoming.* New York: Fawcett Juniper.

Voigt, C. (1982). *Dicey's song.* New York: Atheneum.

Vygotsky, L. S. (1978). *Mind and society.* Cambridge, MA: MIT Press.

Walker, A. (1987). In search of our mothers' gardens. In M. Spring & E. Angeles (Eds.), *Scholastic literature anthologies: Relationships* (pp. 187-189). New York: Scholastic Books.

Weitzman, C. (1975). *My backyard history book.* Boston: Little, Brown & Company.

Wells, G. (2000). Dialogic inquiry in education: building on the legacy of Vygotsky. In C.D. Lee & P. Smagorinsky (Eds.) *Vygotskian perspectives on literacy research.* Cambridge: Cambridge University Press.

White, E. B. (1974). *Charlotte's web.* New York: Harper Trophy.

White, M., Moore, E., & De Regniers, B. (Eds.), (1988). *Sing a song of popcorn: Every child's book of poems.* New York: Scholastic Books.

Whitman, R. (1982). *Becoming a poet.* Boston: The Writer, Inc.

Willis, M. S. (2000). *Personal fiction writing: A guide to writing from real life for teachers, students, and writers.* (Second Edition). New York: Teachers and Writers Collaborative.

Wong, N. (1993). How a girl got her Chinese name. In A. F. Ada, V. J. Harris, and L. B. Hopkins (Eds.). *A chorus of cultures anthology: Developing literacy through multicultural poetry.* Carmel, CA: Hampton-Brown Books.

Worthy, J., Ivey, M., & Broaddus, K. (2001). *Pathways to independence: Reading, writing, and learning in grades 3-8.* New York: The Guilford Press.

Yolen, J. (1987). *Owl moon.* New York: Philomel.

Yolen, J. (1991). The route to story. *The New Advocate, 4,* 143-149.

Yolen, J. (1994, Nov./Dec.). An empress of thieves. *Horn Book Magazine,* 702-705.

Yolen, J. (1995). *Letting swift river go.* Boston: Little Brown.

Zinsser, W. (1987). *Inventing the truth: The art and craft of memoir.* Boston: Houghton Mifflin.